D0922659

THE MEANINGS OF THE MODALS IN PRESENT-DAY AMERICAN ENGLISH

JANUA LINGUARUM

STUDIA MEMORIAE
NICOLAI VAN WIJK DEDICATA

edenda curat

C. H. VAN SCHOONEVELD

INDIANA UNIVERSITY

SERIES PRACTICA

XLV

1966

MOUTON & CO.

THE HAGUE · PARIS

THE MEANINGS OF THE MODALS IN PRESENT-DAY AMERICAN ENGLISH

by

MADELINE ELIZABETH EHRMAN

YALE UNIVERSITY

1966

MOUTON & CO.

THE HAGUE · PARIS

Printed in The Netherlands.

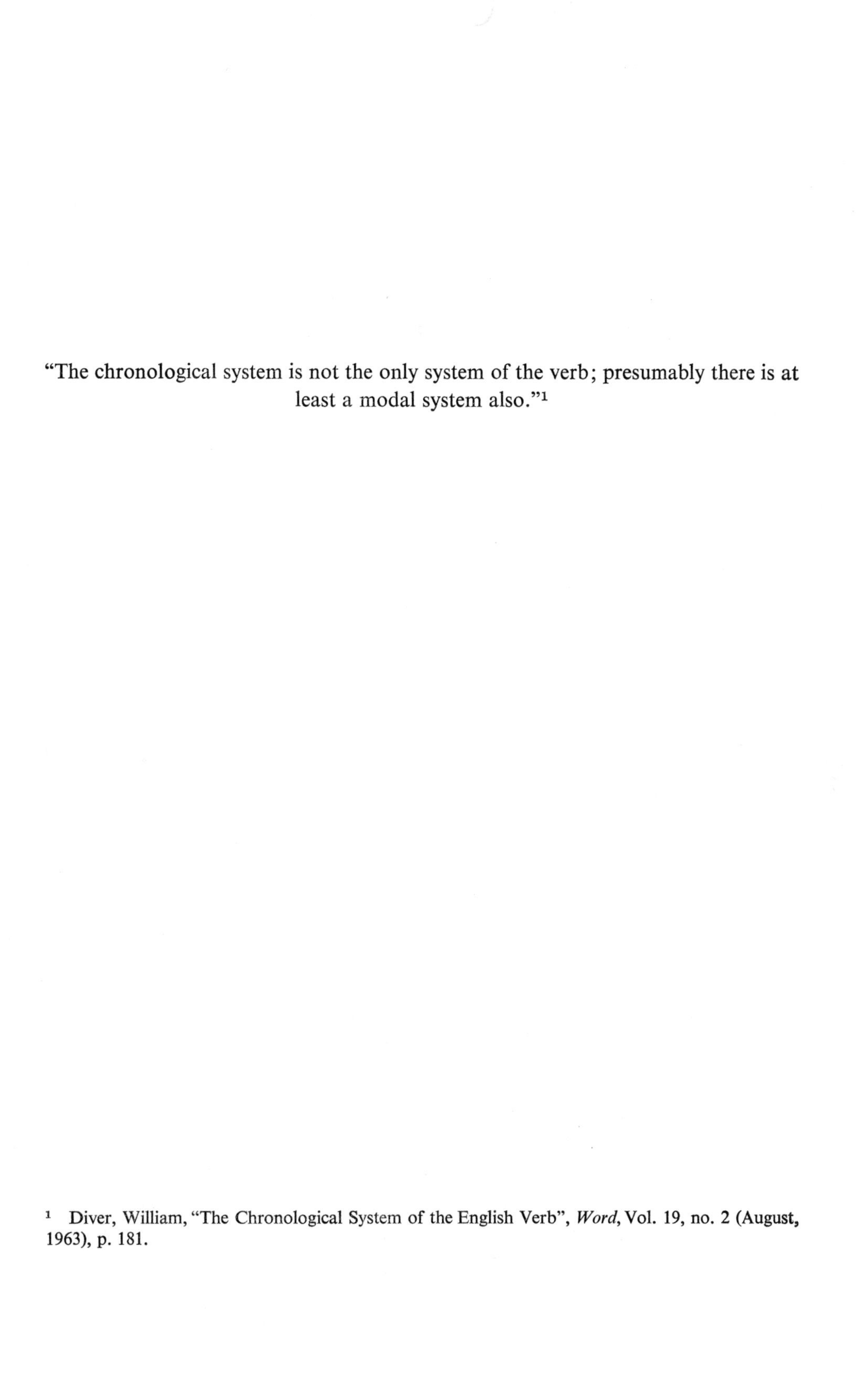

"The chronological system is not the only system of the verb; presumably there is at least a modal system also."[1]

[1] Diver, William, "The Chronological System of the English Verb", *Word*, Vol. 19, no. 2 (August, 1963), p. 181.

TABLE OF CONTENTS

1. INTRODUCTION*

The study which this paper describes began with the question of whether or not Martin Joos' semological classification of the modal auxiliaries in *The English Verb: Form and Meaning* is valid, especially for American English. It was my feeling before beginning, and it is still my feeling, that the idea of symmetrical or exceptionless semantic arrangements has been so appealing to students of the modal auxiliary system that they have tended to overlook arrangements which are less tidy but which perhaps correspond better to present-day usage. It was my desire to determine just what each modal auxiliary means, exactly what it does to the predication of which it is a part; and if a system were to appear in my set of meanings, so much the better. However, if there were to prove to be no orderly, symmetrical system, I would not have considered the work I had done a failure for that reason alone. It happens that a system of three sets of bipolar contrasts does not seem to fit the modal system perfectly, even with inclusion of marginal items like *dare*, *need*, and *shall*. I have arrived at a rather loosely structured set of relationships, which will be presented at the end of this paper. It may not satisfy those who look for more system. I realize that individual usage can vary considerably, depending upon dialect and educational background (*shall* is particularly susceptible to this). However, I hope that my meanings are sufficiently general to cover most of the variations in American standard speech.

Modal auxiliaries are defined for purposes of this study as that closed class of verbs which may occupy the first position of a verb phrase, which may not be immediately preceded by another verb, which may invert with the subject in interrogation, and which are negated directly by *not*. The fact that a modal auxiliary is not immediately preceded by another verb form is crucial; the other characteristics set off *be* and *have* from the other verbs as well. The forms that meet these requirements are *can*, *could*, *may*, *might*, *will*, *would*, *shall*, *should*, *must*, *ought to*, and marginally *dare* and *need*.

My investigation was carried out on the modal auxiliaries from approximately 300,000 running words from the corpus of American English which has been prepared by the Linguistics Department at Brown University. This corpus consists of samples of approximately 2,000 words each from American prose printed in 1961. No text was used which contained more than 50% dialogue. At the time I began, about a third

* The research reported herein was partially supported through the Cooperative Research Program of the Office of Education, U.S. Department of Health, Education, and Welfare.

of the eventual million-word total had been put on tape for computer use. By means of a word-in-context program, each occurrence of a modal auxiliary was extracted with ten to twenty words of context on each side. When the context was not sufficient to determine the meaning, I turned to the larger context contained in the full print-out of the corpus. Location markers following each example identify the line of text in which each modal auxiliary occurs. For the most part I have limited my statements to the material in the corpus; however, I have inconsistently and sporadically made reference to the usage to which I am accustomed in speech if it seemed important at the time.

The following are the forms listed on the program. Those marked with an asterisk did not occur.

will	couldn't	mightn't*	daring
won't	shall	must	ought
would	shan't*	mustn't	oughtn't*
wouldn't	should	dare	need
can	shouldn't	dasn't*	needs
cannot	may	daren't*	needed
can't	mayn't*	dares	needn't*
could	might	dared	needing

In dealing with secondary sources, a representative rather than inclusive group of grammarians, I have confined myself to their comments on the points with which I was myself concerned: meaning, classification of meaning, and those aspects of context which have distinguishable effect on meaning. This last includes tense behavior, other elements of the verb phrase, some other sentence elements, and the overall content of the passage. My primary interest was in the discovery of the most general meaning(s) for each modal auxiliary that would apply to as many occurrences as possible. Meanings conditioned by specific sentence elements and features of nonsemantic interest have generally been distinguished by the term USE, and they have been perhaps less than systematically treated. Those which I discussed appeared within the corpus and were generally dealt with to make distinctions or to illustrate the generality of the basic meaning.

The BASIC MEANING is the most general meaning of the modal in question, the meaning that applies to all its occurrences. In a sense it is the lowest common denominator of all the occurrences, for the determination of which context is unnecessary. There also appear for almost all of the modals what I have perhaps metaphorically called OVERTONES. These are subsidiary meanings which derive from the basic meaning but which add something of their own. No overtone accounts for all the occurrences of a modal (in that case it would be a basic meaning), and all are conditioned by elements of the context which cannot be identified, isolated, and listed. The factors which account for overtone variation are almost certainly from the content of the surroundings.

TIME FUNCTION is used only for *will* and *shall* and refers to a contextually conditioned variation in temporal relationship to the surrounding discourse which affects all overtones and the basic meaning. TEMPORAL FUNCTION, on the other hand, indicates the relation of the time of any modal auxiliary to the time of its utterance or context without reference to the conditioners relevant for time function; i.e. it is the relations of E^nE^n or E^nE^s which Jakobson describes in *Shifters, Verbal Categories, and the Russian Verb*.[1] PREDICTION is used to refer to a guaranteed or assured occurrence without reference to time function; it is the basic meaning of *shall* and *will*. A distinction should be made between the time of the DISCOURSE (the immediately surrounding context) and the time of the UTTERANCE (the moment in which the modal is actually spoken or written).

I have adopted the phrase "state of the world" from Martin Joos (*op. cit.*, preliminary edition), since it is a good way of referring to the environmental qualities which I have subsumed under the heading "conditioner" in Table 3 (p. 76). For the most part, other terms are described and defined in the text.

This monograph is a somewhat revised version of a thesis submitted to Brown University in partial fulfilment of the requirements for the degree of Master of Arts (Department of Linguistics, 1965).

I should like to acknowledge the many debts I have contracted in the production of this study. I am grateful to Professors W. Nelson Francis and W. Freeman Twaddell for suggesting this topic for my thesis, the investigation of which has resulted in my sometimes feeling almost a personal ownership of the English modals. I am also most grateful to Professor Henry Kučera, who, in addition to directing Mr. Stanley Legum in writing the concordance program which provided me with my primary source material, has willingly given me much encouragement and valuable advice.

It is Professor Francis' contribution, however, that I should especially like to acknowledge. Mr. Francis has been unfailingly patient and interested, far exceeding the requirements of his position as my thesis advisor. He has been more than generous with his time, in reading and commenting on my work and in discussing the many points of interest which the investigation raised. There is no portion of this study which does not show his influence. But most of all, I appreciate his warm, invaluable guidance during all the time I have been a student in linguistics.

[1] Jakobson, Roman, *Shifters, Verbal Categories, and the Russian Verb* (Russian Language Project, Department of Slavic Languages and Literatures, Harvard University, 1957).

2. CAN

The basic meaning of *can* is that there is no obstruction to the action of the lexical verb of which *can* is an auxiliary; that is to say, that action is free to take place. Any other meanings of the verb can be derived more or less directly from this basic meaning, though some have developed in such a way that they seem to say the converse, to make an assertion of ability or potentiality. Most of the sentences of the pure basic type do not specify the type of circumstances which permit the action (1), but often they refer to outside factors which could affect the subject of the verb phrase. Frequently, for instance, the implied reference is primarily to physical barriers to the action which happen not to be present, as in sentence (2).

(1)[1] "You *can* get *something*", Nadine would snap. "You *can* get a job working in a grocery store, if nothing else." 1630E1P18

(2) But the shelter is as much a part of my landscape as the beech and horse-chestnut trees that grow on the ridge. I *can* see it from this window where I write. 0080E1K22

Closely related to the basic meaning is a relatively rare one of permission. Seven out of ten occurrences of this meaning variation appear in dialogue as in, for example, sentence (3). The remaining three instances are a clearly permissive statement of regulation (4) and two potentially ambiguous cases (5). The ambiguity of (5) is resolved in the extended context.

(3) Even though this is my rock, you *can* use it sometimes. 1020E1P16

(4) ... or any kind of boat with mechanical propulsion rated at more than 10 horsepower before it *can* be used on Federal waterways. 1200E1E06

(5) You *can* do likewise though Christ is not bodily present. You *can* ignore Him. You *can* ignore His book, the Bible and His church. You *can* laugh at His blood-bought salvation, ... 1440E1D16

There are five examples of a special permissive meaning which makes the permission almost a command, as in (6). All occur in dialogue.

[1] Italics indicate study forms. If they are italicized in the text, underlining is used. Other italicized forms remain.

(6) ". . . I don't know what you're up to, but when Brenner" – "You *can* forget about Brenner, too", Curt said. 0820E1J48

A unique instance in dialogue, (7), involves an enabling of the action through outside circumstances but also through the authority that the speaker has to confirm such facts to the addressee.

(7) "You *can* tell Kayabashi-*san* that the back road is in very good condition and will be quite safe . . ." 0950E1K19

Statements of the ability of the subject of the verb phrase also relate to the basic meaning. *Can* may focus directly on the subject, as in (8) ,which says that there is no lack or deficiency *in the subject* which prevents the action of the verb from taking place. This is very common and may be used with non-personal subjects as well as with personal ones. Sometimes the modal seems to do more than indicate the non-existence of a deficiency; it often seems to point to some aspect of the subject that has a positive effect on the action of the main verb. In sentence (9), for instance, there is more than simply a statement that nothing in the make-up of religion interferes with its summating, epitomizing, etc. The *can* here implies positive qualities of religion as well: there is nothing other than the auxiliary in the sentence which contributes to such an interpretation.

(8) Martin and Stendler present evidence that infants and young children *can* and do solve many problems at a relatively simple perceptual level . . . 0020E1J47

(9) Religion *can* summate, epitomize, relate, and conserve all the highest ideals and values— 0400E1J23

Some of these sentences, in addition to making the meaning of the modal seem somewhat positive in terms of subject's capacity, also include a strong notion of hypothesis and condition carried wholly by the auxiliary (10). In (11) the hypothetical implication is reinforced by the parenthetical element.

(10) Knowing *specifically* what the many feed additives can do and how and when to feed them *can* make a highly competitive business more profitable . . . 0020E1E27

(11) They speak of the work of Christ as the bestowal of incorruptibility, which *can* mean (though it does not have to mean) deliverance from time and history. 1340E1D04

Can may carry heavy overtones of conditionality, especially when the lexical verb is *be*. The modal auxiliary here implies an "if"-clause: circumstances must be right for the bathroom in sentence (12) to be scary.

(12) A dark bathroom *can* be pretty scary, . . . 0250E1P16

Passives bear a similarity to indications of subject capacity in sentences like (8). In passives like (13) there seems to be a reference to some quality in the subject of the passive verb, the object of the verb in the usually impersonal kernel sentence (13a) of which the passive is a transform. The modal in the kernel sentence has the basic meaning.

(13) These engines *can* be removed from a boat with relative ease, . . . 0810E1E06
(13a)[2] One *can* remove these engines from a boat with ease.

Very frequently the context states a factor, quality, or circumstance which seems to actively contribute to the effecting of the action (14). The meaning of the auxiliary remains, in this case, the basic one. However, in a sentence like (15) the meaning of the auxiliary seems to be somewhat more restricted by what is stated elsewhere in the sentence; what it indicates is "given X circumstance(s), nothing stands in the way of the action".

(14) Since the change to better nutrition, he feels he *can* report on improvements in health, . . . 1750E1F04
(15) That way he *can* truck his parts right indoors and unload them under the roof. 0240E1E35

As long as there is another element in the sentence to which such a special meaning can be attributed, we must assume that *can* carries only the basic meaning. Thus the following sentences are examples of special effects of time, through the meaning of the lexical verb (16) and through a subordinate time expression (17). Both give the verb a future reference. An "if"-clause contributes elements of conditionality and often futurity, as in (18).

(16) These societies *can* expect to face difficult times. 0010E1J22
(17) "I *can* fix him something later in the afternoon when we get home." 0330E1K01
(18) "We *can* get it if we dig, . . ." 0390E1N20

Some special sentence effects of considerable interest appear in the case of negation with forms other than "not". This is here called "indirect negation". It includes as the most common forms "only" (adjective and adverb) and "no" (adjective), but other forms of indirect negation also appear in the same clause as the modal auxiliary. "Only" has the effect of limiting the basic meaning of *can*: in sentence (19) and its like the meaning is that all alternatives are barred except the one mentioned. "Nothing . . . but" (20) has the same effect as the "not . . . except" construction of (21). Other indirect negators which limit the meaning of the verb phrase but do not negate it altogether are "little" in two occurrences, "few" in one occurrence, and "least" also in one occurrence. Indirect negation also shows in the case of passives, which re-transform into actives with the negative adjective in the complement (22).

(19) . . . he *can* only conclude that there must have been something "contagious" . . . 1290E1J27

[2] No location marker indicates that the writer has supplied the example.

(20) Tonal morphophonemics, in a common case, *can* do nothing but either raise or lower the tone. 1030E1J34

(21) "... but there's not a blessed thing they *can* do with two or three of us except chase us, ..." 1380E1K09

(22) ... little or no correlation between length and distribution *can* be detected. 1600E1J11

All other forms of indirect negation have the effect of full negation of the basic meaning and are therefore equivalent to *cannot*, though they also have adverbial or adjectival force. This effect is especially clear in the case of adjectival "no" in complement position, where with one exception it always follows copulative "be" (23). The one occurrence of "hardly" also has the effect of full negation (24). There are no instances of a partially negative "hardly" like (24a), which has much the same effect as "only" in that it severely limits the possibility of action.

(23) ... it follows that their image curves *can* have no free intersections. 0650E1J21

(24) "I *can* hardly say the same about you, Dave!" 1130E1P27

(24a) I *can* hardly imagine it.

(25) nothing *can* snow snow but "it". 0610E1J33

Direct negation appears in the form of "can't" and "cannot". There is one instance of "can not", but this looks as if it is equivalent to "cannot", since the sentence makes no sense if the negator affects anything but the modal auxiliary. The negated forms follow much the same pattern as the positive: the great majority are expressive of the basic meaning itself, and of those carrying additional or supplementary meaning, the majority have the first overtone, in which something within the subject seems to participate in the establishment or prevention of freedom of the action of the verb (26). In addition there are three uses of the modal with permissive meaning (but none with a force approaching command) (27), and one which would seem to carry hypothetical force if affirmative (28).

(26) "... I *can't* conceive of her having had a deadly enemy." 1790E1L15

(27) "Stop that! You'll wake up the whole building. Wally *can't* go any place at this hour—" 0860E1P18

(28) "... And also, the money *can't* mean as much to Bobbie, ..." 1580E1P17

The effect of the negation is, of course, to reverse the meaning of the auxiliary and to give the sentence the meaning of "there is something preventing the action of the verb" or "the way is not clear". Usually the agent barring the action is not expressed, but in the case of the above-mentioned overtones it is implied (personal deficiency, another person's legislation) and in some sentences is actually stated by a phrase or a clause in the same or in a neighboring sentence. The feeling of hypothesis which was found in some affirmative sentences differs from the other overtones in that it, as well as the basic meaning, is negated by "not".

Can't and *cannot* are stylistic variants; *can't* appears in dialogue all but four times, while *cannot* is used in dialogue only three times.

Also interesting, however, is that this distinction carries through to other aspects of the language. With *can't* all the subjects but four are personal pronouns (or no subject at all, indicating a first-person subject previously mentioned). Of these four one is "it" and only one other is a non-human noun. On the other hand, the distribution of subjects with *cannot* seems to be an undistinguished mixture of personal and impersonal pronoun and noun subjects like that of affirmative *can.* Also, with the formal negative there are nineteen passives, or almost half the total (almost a quarter of the affirmative sentences are passive), while with the contraction there are no passives at all. Questions occur only with the contraction, and all of them are of the yes-or-no type.

Verb phrases with *can* consist most commonly of the modal auxiliary plus the unmarked infinitive of the lexical verb. The most frequent of the fuller verb phrases is, as mentioned above, the passive construction. Others are extremely rare: there is one instance of phase[3] (29) and one of aspect (30). Otherwise verb phrases with *can* are very uncomplex.

(29) Poor devil he *can't* have been too happy either. 1050E1K18

(30) I *can* be working at it, and keep an eye on the baby and the stove at the same time. 0800E1P02

For all the modal auxiliaries, it is understood that the meaning of the word includes the fact that any statement it makes is dependent upon the speaker's or writer's view of the state of the world. In some cases this view will be seen to be an important contrastive marked feature of meaning or overtone.

COULD

The meanings of *could* as a modal auxiliary are essentially the same as those of its "present" or "non-past" form *can.* That is, they all have the basic meaning of "there is nothing in the state of the world preventing the action of the verb", or, in the case of the negatives, that there is some such barring factor. The basic meaning without overtones is as usual overwhelmingly the most common use.

(31) I sat where I *could* watch the exit . . . 0790E1L02

Most of the overtones described for *can* occur in approximately the same proportions as before; that is, the most frequent is that of capacity or qualities in the subject of the

[3] The effect of phase marking will be discussed in the treatment of *could.*

verb phrase which remove barriers to action (32). The next in frequency of occurrence is the permissive overtone. There is only one occurrence of the permissive overtone with the strong suggestion of almost imperative force which was noted above (33), and there are no occurrences at all of the yet rarer occurrential overtone of condition or hypothesis. Of course, this last overtone is not necessary in view of the function of past modification on the verb form.

(32) She always *could* sense the shag end of a woolly day. 0960E1P27
(33) She said what she meant and let it be . . . He *could* take the advice or leave it. 0700E1P27

Indirect negation and direct negation continue, as before, to indicate the opposite of the basic meaning. The overtones resulting from internal qualities and from permission are both found here, but as always the primary and most common meaning is the basic one (34), (35), (36). It is always the meaning of *can* that is negated; the results of past-tense modification remain unaffected by negation. As in the case of *can*, "not" never affects any portion of the verb phrase other than the modal auxiliary.

(34) . . . it is unlikely that a planned episode *could* be initiated. 1520E1J08
(35) It was not exactly panic they gave way to, but they *could* not just sit there. 1510E1K05
(36) . . . and there were no chairs and you *couldn't* smoke and the cooling was overhead fans . . . 1520E1P09

Couldn't appears 86 times, of which two are passive and three are propredicates. *Could* with any other kind of negation appears passively in 16 out of 67 negated examples. Of the 86 occurrences of *couldn't* only 18 appear in dialogue, and two of these are in indirect discourse form. While this seems to conflict with the findings for *can't*, at the same time it is possible to note that all the non-dialogue occurrences of *couldn't* are in fictitious narrative, which is often in the first person. Indeed, most of the other occurrences of *could* are from fiction; factual sources are considerably fewer than for *can*. It might, then, be concluded that there is some stylistic difference between *can* and *could* – primarily the fact that as a rule only narrative (usually fictional) appears in the past, though there are some few instances of factual articles written in past narrative (38).

With the exception of 19 human noun subjects (37), two cases of subject "it", one inanimate noun subject, and the two passives, all the rest of the instances of *couldn't* have a personal pronoun as subject. This corresponds with the findings for *can't*.

(37) "Mrs. Roberts had called and *couldn't* wake you. . . ." 0350E1P18
(38) The cathode consisted of a ¼″ diameter thoriated tungsten rod attached to a water cooled copper tube. This tube *could* be adjusted in its axial direction . . . 0740E1J02

The past tense contrasts with the other facet of *could*, the meaning of the verb itself, in that it has a very definite and separate effect on the meaning of the verb phrase. The most common reason for past modification is the rule of sequence of tense; this may be caused by a preceding verb form in the past (39), and this verb may be another past modal auxiliary. Use of the past form is frequently forced by indirect discourse, in which the verb of discourse (the forcing verb) is in the past (40).

(39) He stood up, stretched, looked around for the bubbles, but *could* see none.
0940E1L19

(40) . . . he knocked on their door and asked if there was anything he *could* do for them.
0590E1K13

The verb forcing past modification need not always precede the modal auxiliary or even occur in the same or immediately preceding sentence. In some cases the preceding past verb is separated from the modal in question by a direct quote in the present (41). Such a case is illustrative of the force sequence-of-tense rules can have, even when it is sequence within the broader discourse and not within the narrower confines of the sentence containing the modal or of the immediately preceding sentence.

(41) ". . . I'll shoot the first man who doesn't." I *could* see them in my sights.
0870E1N04

This is by far the greatest category into which the past modification falls. However, although in many of these cases the past verb refers to past action, as long as a past form is forced by the rules of sequence of tenses, be it close or loose, past time cannot be considered part of the contrastive meaning of the modification any more than futurity could be described as part of the meaning of *can* before the lexical verb "expect to". To the writer's surprise there were only two instances where prior time constituted the meaning of the past modification portion of the significance of *could.* This was in instances where all that preceded had been in the non-past, and the past modal auxiliary opened a somewhat new temporal function describing an earlier state of affairs or referred to a prior series of activities. There were no other forms of *could* referring purely to previous time.

(42) Similar findings have been noted in a patient with congenital absence of the organification enzymes, whose thyroid tissue *could* only concentrate iodide.
0430E1J14

When Martin Joos gives what is normally known as "past tense" the name "remote tense",[4] he is in a sense saying that the quality of remoteness either from the moment of speech or from the actual reality discernible at that moment is the primary constituent of the meaning of this portion of the verb-phrase tagmeme. It is only this factor which can ally the meaning of previous time with which we have just been concerned with the other meaning of non-actuality (i.e., remoteness from immediately

[4] Joos, p. 24, preliminary edition.

perceptible reality). Non-actuality occurs in several forms, of which the first and most frequent is hypothesis. Hypothesis is almost always tinged with an implied condition or "if"-clause, as in (43); in (44) a stated "if"-clause is illustrated.

(43) Equivalents *could* be assigned to the paradigm either at the time it is added to the dictionary or after the word has been studied in context. 1580E1J32
(44) . . . and if looks *could* kill, Wally would have been dead. 0620E1P18

Considerably less frequent is the non-actual derivative meaning of "contrary-to-fact", which occurs only after "if", "as if", and statements of wish, as in (45). Also infrequent is the polite use of the past forms which, as George Curme puts it, indicate that the speaker is not counting on fulfillment of his wish, thus avoiding a blunt expression of will. This is what Curme calls the "subjunctive of modest wish".[5] As long as this politeness derives from the non-actual meaning of past modification, it cannot be considered a separate meaning any more than could the overtone of permission to the basic meaning of *can*. Indeed, in sentences like (46) there is so much of both hypothesis and of politeness that one could hesitate to make a distinction, or at least one could consider the polite past a use conditioned by context to a greater extent than the other effects of the past. Sentences like (46) show that the contrary is the case: non-actuality is retained because "modest wish" is not a meaning but a function, and non-actuality is the meaning of the past tense here. Politeness occurs in addition to unreality, not instead of it.

(45) . . . during which he studied Scotty's face as if Scotty were not there and *could* not study him too, . . . 1650E1K01
(46) ". . . *Could* you possibly have lunch with him today? His car *could* pick you up at your hotel at twelve." 1520E1L01

All six clearly polite uses occur in dialogue; of these, three are requests (47) and one is a statement of fact in which the past modal clearly has the function of reducing peremptoriness (48). In none of them could the writer see evidence for Curme's statement that "Here the past tense forms lose in large measure the element of unreality . . ."[6]

(47) He asked, "*Could* we have a drink?" 0480E1N01
(48) As cheerfully as possible, he said, "Well, I guess we *could* all do with a little drink." 0190E1N20

All the examples discussed so far have occurred either in a present-tense setting or in direct quotes, which are not affected by sequence of tense rules. As a result the meanings and functions of the past tense have been reasonably unambiguous. However, every one of the non-actual meanings or overtones also appears in a situation such that it is not clear whether the meaning to be ascribed is due to sequence of tenses

[5] Curme, p. 391.
[6] Curme, p. 391.

(that is, probably the entire context carries a meaning of previous time) or non-actuality. An example of such ambiguous sentences, which are very common, is item (49). This is a sentence which, if made into a direct quote, could retain the past form, so it seems likely that in most such cases there may be little real ambiguity – past tense is forced by sequence of tense rules, with the result that the meaning of the past is non-actuality.

(49) The Vice President had called and asked if he *could* see the Secretary at his home. 1110E1K03

In a sentence like (50) there is an ambiguity which is quite genuine. This sentence could mean either "she was not prevented from killing" – that is, it is past *only* because it follows a past verb and not because of non-actuality – or it could have the conditional, hypothetical meaning which it would probably have if it were a direct, present-tense quote: "In the state she is in, she could actually kill him."

(50) I was plenty scared. In the state she was in, she *could* actually kill him! 0760E1P18

Sometimes, to be sure, this kind of ambiguity is handled by context. Occasionally, however, phase serves to relieve ambiguity. It may appear with negation of all kinds. "Have" after *could* has several effects, of which the most expectable is, surprisingly, the rarest. Without a modal auxiliary the effect of auxiliary "have" in a verb phrase is described by both Twaddell[7] and Joos[8] as "current relevance", but with *could* this is the primary effect of "have" in only one sentence (51). The most common effect of "have" is to put the verb phrase unambiguously in the past. Examination of the great majority of verb phrases with marked phase shows that where the non-actual meaning of the past modal is that of contrary-to-fact, the effect of "have" is always to put the time of that particular verb's action before the time of another, which may be either another expressed verb (52) (time of discourse) or the utterance itself (53) (time of utterance).

(51) They were both so young, after all, so unready for any final parting. How *could* it have been thirty years already, she wondered? 1580E1K25
(52) Going downstairs with the tray, Winston wished he *could* have given in to Miss Ada, but he knew better than to do what she said . . . 0010E1K28
(53) "I'd give anything if I *could* have found a girl like you." 1210E1K26

Most frequently the *could* used with "have" is hypothetical, reflecting the situation found for ordinary verb phrases consisting of modal auxiliary plus lexical verb. When the meaning is that of hypothesis, the effect of "have" is also primarily one of

[7] Twaddell, p. 2. I have also adopted the term "modification" from Twaddell to refer to phase, aspect, and voice marking.
[8] Joos, p. 25, preliminary edition.

putting the normally ambiguous modal into the past – it is close to the effect of "have" with contrary-to-fact *could.*

(54) The girl, her first, she barely remembered. It *could* have been anyone's infant, for it had not survived the bassinet. 0870E1K23

(55) If she *could* have blushed, she would have. 0880E1M05

This effect on ambiguity may perhaps be explained as follows. If "have" were not present in the verb phrase, the past modal could refer to a period of time unspecified as to both occurrence and to duration, but when "have" is introduced it always adds the factor of localization to a specific place in the narrative or sequence of events. Instead of serving as a statement of a state of affairs with little relevance to time, when phase is introduced the verb phrase generally comes to describe a single episode or event. This effect is particularly well illustrated by sentence (56).

(56) I think you *could* have heard him a mile away, . . . 0080E1K09

With *could* there also appear two expressed instances of a verb phrase containing aspect (but not phase) and one instance of aspect-marking in a propredicate where *could* is implied (57); however, in contrast to "have", "be + -ing" seems to have no relation at all to the meaning of the modal auxiliary.

(57) . . . and chattering about how she *could* put up a typewriter right there, and be brushing up on her typing so Eugenia wouldn't be ashamed of it. 0780E1P02

Suprasegmentals are, of course, not indicated in writing, with the exception of the two italicized examples of *could* and two of *can.* Of course with the present tense form italicization serves to emphasize its meaning, but in the past example it seems to serve to emphasize the hypothetical meaning of past modification (58).

(58) ". . . After all, I didn't know you, Pete. It *could* have have been an accident." 1620E1L23

The situation for *can/could* is, then, that there is one basic meaning for *can* – that nothing in the state of the world stands in the way of the action of the verb of which *can* is an auxiliary. Frequently it happens that other connotations are attached to the modal, some of which can be explained by the presence of other expressed factors in the sentence or context, such as the lexical verb itself. Those which cannot have been referred to as "overtones". They are really all specific derivatives of the basic meaning whose use is conditioned by context elements which cannot be isolated.

When *can* appears in the past, its meaning must be segmented into two portions, of which the first is that of *can* itself and the second is that of the past tense. The latter may be either past time or non-actuality. If the past tense is forced by sequence of tense rules, a meaning of past time may not be necessary but may still be assumed. Sometimes it is not clear whether the meaning of a past form is an environmental one of past time or whether it is non-actuality, but such ambiguity may be cleared by use of phase modification.

3. MAY

In contrast to *can*, which has a single meaning discernible in all uses, *may* is somewhat more complicated. Instead of having a unitary meaning, *may* is defined in terms of a continuum characterized by two dimensions of meaning. The first of these corresponds very closely with the meaning of *can* (nothing prevents the predication); indeed, at one extreme of the continuum for this dimension, which can be called "circumstance", there seems to be very little difference between *can* and the *may* that is actually used. Certainly in a case like (59) the implication of *nihil obstat* is dominant beyond doubt.

(59) ... [the] distribution obtained from visual and radar observations of meteors *may* be extrapolated to the micrometeorite domain. 0510E1J07

The overtones described for *can* appear here for *may* as well, which is not surprising in view of the fact that the meaning of *can* is always either a part of the meaning of *may* or else is implied by it. In sentence (60) the old overtone of subject potential appears in the use of *may* (this particular sentence, by the way, is unlike (59) in that it is not as near the end of the scale of meaning dominated by circumstance).

(60) The following generalizations about the emotional characteristics of elementary-school children *may* be helpful. 0250E1J47

There is quite a range of permissive uses. Beginning with sentences like (59), permission first seems to enter when the sentence is such that it is necessary to assume that the reason there is no obstruction to the verbal action is that something else, usually an artificial set of rules, or preestablished facts, as in (62), has so structured circumstance. The set of rules, axioms, or facts is not the subject of the verb phrase, and in a sense it may be felt as "permitting" the predication. This kind of permission occurs very frequently in mathematical and in some technical texts.

(61) The points *may* also touch C without crossing. 0260E1J20
(62) The recommended 10-milligram daily intake level should be maintained. It *may* be incorporated into cattle creep feeds in levels from 1.0 to 1.5 milligrams ... per pound ... 0930E1E27

Another transitional permissive is exemplified by (63), in which the agency in which we are interested is impersonal but nonetheless concrete and based on human decree.

In (64), the authority is a ruling (as opposed to an axiomatic "rule") based on human decision. Needless to say, the next step is direct human authority (65).

(63) You *may* have your boat of wood, canvas, plywood, plastic, or metal. 0620E1E06

(64) . . . so is the carefree attitude toward what a boatman *may* and *may* not do; must and should do. 1100E1E06

(65) I should be obliged if you could make other arrangements for your daughters. You *may* stay as long as you wish, of course, . . . 0230E1K23

As in the case of *can*, permission seems to assume imperative force in some few (here two) instances (66). Sentence (67) looks very much like a normal-sentence-order statement of the old "indirect imperative"[1] ("May you soon know . . ."), of which no examples at all occurred in the sample.

(66) . . . the development of our present scientific view of the world for which we *may* be rightly grateful. 0410E1D01

(67) Perhaps you do not know if you belong to Him. You *may* know that you are in God's family and be just as sure of it as you are that you belong to the family of your earthly father. 1070E1D06

The remaining overtone of *can*, condition or hypothesis, retains its anomalous character by being characteristic of *may* at the other end of the scale, which is dominated by the second dimension of "occurrence". It is this dimension which always, in some way or other, accounts for the difference between *can* and *may* in its most circumstantial uses, for non-hypothetical *can* refers only to circumstance – whether the action occurs or not is of no relevance. On the contrary, *may* always refers to an openness to occurrence (i.e., there is no guarantee that the action did not, will not, or is not taking place). Even in (59), where the similarity to *can* is one of the closest in the entire corpus, the residue of difference, if any, has to be the slight element of openness to occurrence which *may* confers. Subtraction of the meaning of *can*, that is, leaves only a residue consisting of elements of the occurrence dimension.

In (68) *may* and *can* actually appear in the same sentence. The contrast makes the difference in meanings clear, for this *can* is a prime example of the basic meaning, while *may*, if it is not considered permissive, emphasizes the dimension of occurrence which gives it its meaning by contrast (and in connection with a special concessive use which will be discussed later).

(68) Actually, all a man in uniform has to do is to get by. He *may* not rise to the heights, but he *can* get by, and eventually be retired. 1540E1P05

The two continua, circumstance and occurrence, are such, then, that they vary inversely. At the end where the meaning of *can* is strong, that of openness to occurrence is weak (but always present), and vice versa.

[1] Long, p. 136.

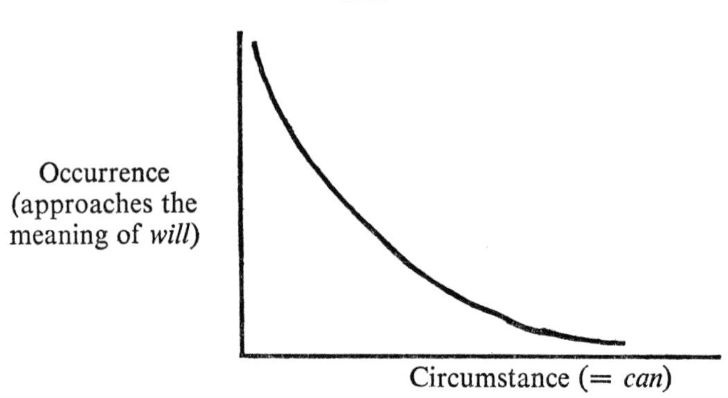

Because of this inverse relationship, it is convenient to refer to *may* as appearing on only one scale of value, but it must always be remembered that there are two dimensions to the scale, both of which are evidenced in any use of the modal auxiliary, no matter how slightly. The dimensions may be represented as axes of a coordinate system, and the meaning of *may* can be represented as a curve of some sort. Since each meaning component approaches but does not reach zero at the other end of the continuum, the curve is similar to a hyperbola.[2]

There are many instances where circumstance clearly participates in the meaning of the occurrence-weighted modal, such as (69), but there are many more where it is simply implied, as in (70). That is, it is necessary that nothing prevent the speculations from having merit before there is any possibility that they *will* have such merit, but this absence of prevention does not appear to be directly expressed in this sentence. In some cases the circumstantial sense, while it can be interpreted into *may*, is of almost total irrelevance. In (71) whether or not the speaker will take his trip is the dimension on which the sentence focuses almost all the reader's attention, and the meaning of *can*, while a premise of the occurrence of the action, is not felt as part of the meaning.

(69) A prospective industry also *may* be interested in the long-run advantages of training programs in the area . . . 0890E1J38

(70) Some of these speculations *may* have some merit, others are somewhat ambiguous. 0690E1J27

(71) On Thursday evening we *may* go out of town together by some stage or mail . . . 0170E1K20

Finally, then, we can return to that last, anomalous overtone of *can*: the conditional or hypothetical. This overtone seems to correspond nearly to *may* at the occurrence-strong end of the general scale; in (72) substitution of such an instance of *can* would make little or no difference to the meaning of the sentence.

[2] I owe this suggestion to Mr. Francis.

(72) The child with high anxiety *may* first direct his . . . energy toward achievement' . . . 1670E1J29

(72a) The child with high anxiety *can* first direct his . . . energy toward achievement, . . .

Although as has been seen this overtone does not appear with *could* because of the functions of the past on that modal auxiliary, some few of the examples of occurrence-strong *may* would retain their meaning better if *could* were substituted rather than conditional *can*. Thus, because in sentence (72) the basic meaning of *can* is irrelevant, the reinforced hypothetical force of the past form would be superfluous, indeed excessive, if the substitution were made as in sentence (72a). In (73), since the meaning of absence of prevention appears close to the surface of *may*, reinforced *could* should be used (73a) to relieve what would probably be an ambiguity if *can* were used (73b). *May* in sentence (74) carries meanings from both dimensions in close to equal proportions. *Could* should be used so that both dimensions can remain almost equally represented, without ambiguity (74a).

(73) In such circumstances, it *may* well be to the advantage of the industry to allow an increase in the basic wage . . . 0720E1J41

(73a) . . . it *could* be to the advantage of the industry to allow an increase . . . (compare with (73) without "well")

(73b) . . . it *can* be to the advantage of the industry to allow an increase. . . (compare with (73) without "well")

(74) This *may* be because the Athabascan divergence began earlier; . . . 0040E1J35

(74a) This *could* be because the Athabascan divergence began earlier; . . .

So far discussion has been limited to the extremes of the scale. However, most of the occurrences appear somewhere between the extremes, as one would expect. Sentence (75) is as good an example as any of a sentence occupying the center position. In (76), the second *may* is considerably closer to the occurrence-weighted end of the scale than the first *may* is, thus illustrating another effect of the variable meaning of this modal auxiliary.

(75) Communication *may* be facilitated by means of the high visibility within the larger community. 1390E1J25

(76) They *may* be related to mental immaturity or lack of aptitude for certain types of school work. The curriculum *may* be too difficult for some and too easy for others. 1410-20E1J47

Needless to say, with such possibility of variation in meaning, ambiguity in individual sentences will be fairly frequent. Usually the ambiguity is between a circumstance-heavy interpretation and a more-or-less balanced one, as in (77). Also common is a confusion between the balanced meaning and the specialized permission-by-fact-oraxiom extension of the circumstance-heavy *may* (78). Permission of human-based agency may also be so confused. Rarely the occurrence-heavy meaning may be confused with the balanced one (79). In (81), on the other hand, any possibility of such ambiguity is specifically averted by the statement "it is permitted", which puts this squarely at the circumstance extreme. Conversely, in (80), not only is the modal auxiliary ambiguous, but its ambiguity is relevant to the syntactic behavior of the rest of the verb phrase. Thus if *may* has the balanced meaning the verb phrase is a copula plus predicate adjective, but if it has a more circumstance-loaded meaning, the verb phrase is a passive construction.

(77) This the therapist *may* pursue in later questioning. 1480E1F01
(78) ... dominant stress *may* or *may* not be on the adjunct *emotionally.* 0380E1J33
(79) ... and evening extension courses also *may* be conducted. 0760E1J38
(80) This exception *may* be connected with Hoijer's use of a much higher percentage of verbs: ... 0420E1J35
(81) (You *may* do as you please)[3] with God now. It is permitted. 1365E1D16

There is one sentence (82) which may be read in three different ways: it may be relatively balanced; it may be very close to the basic meaning of *can*, or it may be permissive by virtue of a previously established set of rules.

(82) In general, any outcome we choose *may* be labeled "success". 0270E1J19

Such ambiguity demonstrates that too sharp a segmentation of the continuum is not likely to be accurate. On the other hand, the ambiguity rather supports the notion of a bipolar range of meaning for *may*, since the frequency of the ambiguities described above could be possible only if the meaning of *may* did not have to be so strictly and narrowly defined as, say, that of *can*, but could occur in several different but interrelated meanings. Otherwise *may* would either have to rely more heavily on other context elements for its definition or it would lose its usefulness because of the several incompatible ambiguities resulting. With a continuum all the meanings of a sentence having as many as three different interpretations, (82) for instance, are compatible and related.

The meaning of *may* as a permissive is, as has been seen, very much at the circumstance-strong end of the scale, to the point where occurrence is hard to detect. A certain separation between the permissive and the other meanings is supported by corresponding behavior of the direct negative with "not". Only where the meaning is permissive does the "not" negate the modal auxiliary (64). In all other cases "not" negates the remainder of the verb phrase and the modal auxiliary remains affirmative, with emphasis on the occurrence dimension of its meaning. It is, of course, relevant that "not" always negates *can*, never the rest of the predicate; that is, it is not surprising that the negator behaves similarly for those meanings of *may* which most closely approximate the meaning of *can*.

[3] The portion in parentheses was printed in small capital letters.

Sentences like (78) really contain two affirmative modal auxiliaries, of which the first is a propredicate construction which would be filled by the verb phrase following "not".

There are three fairly common uses of *may* which rely on separate sentence elements in combination with the modal auxiliary to achieve their effects. The first of these is one which I call "distributive". It occurs with indefinites like "whatever" (83) (also concessive), "which" in indirect questions, or "various" (84). These combine with an occurrence-heavy meaning to give an increased feeling of indefiniteness to the predication.

(83) ... whatever bits or shreds of previous conceptions one *may* find in it, Utopian communism remains ... original – a new thing. 1510E1J57

(84) ... answers do not reveal the different shades of opinion that the various respondents *may* have. 0220E1J45

The next use is one of subordination occurring after "in order that" and equivalent "that" and may be called "purpose". Of the five examples of this in the sample, three are Biblical quotations, one is from a religious tract whose language imitates that of the King James Bible (85), and only one occurs in a secular text (86). This last is one of the mathematics texts, which prove to be conservative in use of *shall* as well.

(85) Intercede for our separated brethren, that with us in the one true fold they *may* be united to the chief Shepherd, the vicar of thy Son. 1180E1D03

(86) ... in order that the assumptions underlying the equations *may* be explicit. 0350E1J41

The third and most frequent use is the concessive, which occurs with several different conjunctions. There are a few examples of "while" and "(even) though" opening the clause in which *may* is used (87), but by far the greatest number of examples appears with a "but" introducing the clause which states the contradiction to the concession (68). In both this and the preceding use, *may* has strong occurrence-loading to its meaning, which sometimes, as has been already mentioned, corresponds to conditional *can.*

(87) Even though the registers *may* have an incomplete record of persons present in a particular area... 1730E1J26

With passives the most frequent meaning of *may* is at the circumstance end of the scale. Occasionally there is a balanced meaning.

May is seldom used in dialogue. It frequently appears in religious and technical texts but not in fiction. There are no cases of aspect with *may*, but there are ten of phase, the effect of which is to put the verb phrase into past time (time anterior to that of the discourse or utterance in which *may* is used) (88). The auxiliary itself is usually time-neutral[4] but in some cases, e.g. (89), it can have a future reference. Such cases are always tied to an occurrence-heavy meaning, but conversely, such meanings do not always have future reference (it can be said that there seems to be some correlation between time function and irrelevance of the meaning of *can* to the meaning of *may* – understandable in view of the fact that the verb when at this end of the scale is already focusing attention on whether or not the predication will take place).

(88) No records are available as to the date or extent of installation, but it *may* have been in 1896. 1530E1J56
(89) We *may* take her with us – to California. 0530E1N02

We have seen, then, that the meaning of *may* is essentially "nothing prevents the action of the predicate, and, what is more, there is no guarantee against the occurrence of that action". Each portion of this definition constitutes a dimension (circumstance or occurrence) in continuum form, and any given example of *may* can be located on these continua. Because the two dimensions are in inverse relation to each other, it is convenient to speak of a single scale of meaning in which there is some element of each dimension, even if it is very slight at the extremes.

A close relation with *can* is necessitated by the inclusion of its meaning in that of *may*; if it is not an active portion of the meaning it is usually implied, and at the circumstantial extreme of the scale, in the permissions, it constitutes practically the entire meaning. As a result *can* is frequently used colloquially in requests, and in careful use *may* assumes connotations of superior social level (from the clear exercise of authority which permission entails). This honorific force of *may* results in its use when permission is being granted only in response to a request originally using *may* or when the speaker wishes to assert his authority. Otherwise the preferred use in speech is the more modest *can* (but those who wish to avoid appearing undereducated often resort to the circumlocution "is it all right if. . ."). On the other hand, perhaps *can* is to some extent moving into the territory of *may* with the occurrential-hypothetical overtone. The relation between occurrence-loaded *may* and *can* has already been discussed. Both forms seem to be almost equally frequent, so these data cannot be used as the basis for a statement on whether one is replacing the other.

MIGHT

In investigating the meaning of *might* a separation between the meaning of *may* and the effects of the past tense is assumed. The result is a somewhat more complex but still essentially similar situation to that of *could*, wherein each occurrence is classified by the meaning it would have if it were in the present tense (*may*) and also by what the

[4] Time function is discussed in detail under *will*, for which it constitutes an important dimension of meaning.

past modification means. It is in the interactions between the two elements that the complication will be found, rather than in the details of the separate classifications, both of which operate much as they did for *can*.

Most of the range of meaning previously established for *may* appears with *might*. The exception is a total absence of permissive meanings of any sort, representing the circumstantial extreme of the scale. In addition, there are relatively very few of the uses where circumstance is more or less dominant; that is, of 229 total occurrences of *might*, only twenty are clearly expressive of a meaning to the effect that nothing prevents the predication, with the corresponding relative unimportance of the occurrence dimension (90). Of these twenty, two appear in the idiom "might as well".

(90) It *might* be pointed out that the integrating function of religion, for good or ill, has often supported... 1720E1J23

In a few of the twenty the modal auxiliary can also be interpreted as having a balanced meaning, as in (91). The balanced meaning accounts for somewhat fewer than half the total meanings, which gives it a lower frequency than it had with *may*. On the other hand, the occurrence-weighted meaning appears considerably more often with *might* than it did in the case of *may* (92). However, there are only about ten instances of the extreme at the occurrence end of the scale, where the meaning of *can* is not only inactive but is also quite irrelevant, as in (93).

(91) There was only one place where the mountain *might* receive her – 0400E1N08
(92 Because he spoke openly with what Channing had prophesied someone *might* – with daring hyperbole – Parker vindicated Channing's further prophecy...[5] 1280E1D05
(93) She had skipped her lunch hour in the fear that he *might* call while she was out. 1030E1L10

The meanings of the past modification are the same as they were in the case of *could*. The meanings of non-actuality all appear, including hypothesis (94), contrary-to-fact (with phase only) (95), and, very rarely, politeness or modest wish (96). Sequence-of-tense effects appear in the majority of the sentences, but there are no cases here where sequence-of-tense or past-time is the only reason for use of *might* rather than *may* as it often was for *could*. Conversely, of course, sentence (94) exemplifies the not-uncommon occurrence of non-reality without sequence-of-tense.

(94) He reasons that as anacondas 30 feet long are often found, some *might* be 38, ... 1050E1J11
(95) When they got home Harold ... thought how, under different circumstances, they *might* have stayed on here, ... 1370E1K13
(96) You *might* try looking into his wife too. 0050E1L10

[5] This is a confusing sentence. It is to be interpreted that Channing had prophesied that someone might speak with daring hyperbole, and "he" fulfilled the prophecy by so speaking.

Because *might* cannot be used for past time only – it always expresses non-actuality, whether or not sequence-of-tense effects permit a possible past-time interpretation in addition – *can* is again tied to *may*. This time it is because *could* must be used for the past of most of the circumstantial appearances of *may*. This is well exemplified by some changes one could make in sentence (97) producing sentences (97a) and (97b). If *may* is substituted for non-actual *might* (which carries a more or less balanced meaning), the verb phrase falls at the circumstance-heavy end of the continuum (97a). To retain this circumstantial meaning in a past-tense form, we have had to resubstitute *could* in (97b).

(97) . . . radiation is in reasonable agreement with the thermal radiation which *might* be predicted on the basis of the known temperature of Mars. 0340E1J01

(97a) . . . radiation is in reasonable agreement with the thermal radiation which *may* be predicted. . .

(97b) . . . radiation is in reasonable agreement with the thermal radiation which *could* be predicted.

Martin Joos has said much the same thing about the necessary non-actuality of *might*.[6] The only exceptions to this rule are permissive *might*, which usually appears in indirect discourse and past sequence (e.g. "He said I might come") and of which there are no examples in the corpus used, and a few sentences such as (98), where both the meaning of *may* and the effects of the past may be interpreted in more than one way. In such sentences it appears that if the meaning of *may* is balanced, both sequence of tense and hypothesis can be effects of the past. However, it is also possible to interpret the *might* as being circumstance-heavy. In this case the only effect of the past is that of sequence-of-tense, and non-actuality cannot participate without forcing the modal auxiliary to assume the balanced meaning.

(98) He studied the problem for a few seconds and thought of a means by which it *might* be solved. 0520E1N12

The fact that sequence-of-tense *might* can always be interpreted as a non-actual past as well (it is almost always hypothetical) is part of the peculiar relation between past tense and the meaning of *may* itself. While, as described above, *might* retains most of the range of meaning of *may*, in most cases when the past-tense element is introduced the combination of non-actuality and whatever element of the occurrence dimension there is puts the meaning of *might* farther along the scale in the direction of occurrence. Thus the balanced meaning becomes occurrence-weighted, and ordinary occurrence-weighted modals approach the pole of the scale. Meanings which fall at the circumstance-heavy end when non-past approach a more balanced meaning.

This is, of course, because the circumstantial element comes to be outweighed in proportion to the amount of occurrence that originally appeared in the present-tense

[6] Joos, p. 40, preliminary edition.

form. Hypothesis, after all, is quite close in meaning to "there is no guarantee against the occurrence of the predication". Because there was seldom anything of that sort in *can*, it is not surprising that a strict separation of functions could be made for *could*. However, for *might*, while the separation can be made for the sake of consistency, it is somewhat artificial in that it is based on a subtraction of the meaning of the underlying *may*. Thus the total meaning is really heavily weighted by the combined effects of original meaning and meaning of the past. Determination of the proportional roles of occurrence and non-actuality is practically impossible.

A sentence like (97) illustrates the simple non-actual use of *might* in a present-tense environment with no confusion about the effects of the past tense. However, when in a past environment *might* may also be influenced by sequence-of-tense effects of possible past time. Part of the ambiguity of a sentence like (98) can be alleviated in much the same way as it was in the case of *could* – by phase modification. The effect of phase is, in all but a few cases, to put the action of the verb phrase in which it appears into a time anterior to that of the main portion of the context (99). This is true both for hypothetical and for contrary-to-fact *might*, and it is well illustrated in sentences like (100), where the pluperfect "had" in parallel non-modal verb phrases has the same function.

(99) Arthur Williams had to be located, they agreed. He *might* have been in collusion with Johnston on the fraud; ... 0410E1L15

(100) All of it *might* have been heroic, but they had done it in the wrong place. 0860E1P08

The meaning of "have" without a modal auxiliary, current relevance, appears frequently with *might*, but it is always auxiliary to the primary past-time effect, both in present-tense and in past-tense contexts (101). It, too, may appear with both hypothetical and contrary-to-fact past.

(101) She *might* now have taken it away again... Heaven knew... 1000E1L14

Very rarely there appears a verb phrase with phase modification putting it anterior to some event outside the context. For instance, in sentence (102) there is an implied "before what I have to say was called to his attention" in the contrary-to-fact verb phrase, and it is this unstated act of telling before which the act of expecting occurs.

(102) It is at this point in his life that the mature Prokofieff emerges. One *might* have expected that such a violent epoch of transition would have destroyed... 0710E1E22

There is one other unique instance of *might* plus phase. In sentence (103) "have" does not put the verb phrase into a time before that of the surrounding discourse nor does it perfectivize it. It gives it no feeling of current relevance in addition to what a verb phrase without "have" would contain; indeed it seems to be almost completely equivalent in meaning to the simpler "might be mad". The only function it can possibly have is to eliminate any ambiguity that the timeless *might* could have – that is, we can say that it puts the verb phrase into a time anterior to that of the actual act of speaking or writing in which the narrator tells us about the actions. In other words, in this case it is really a special instance of the effect of "have" that was discussed in the preceding paragraph.

(103) ... stood a shape with a sheet or a tarpaulin draped over it. These shapes *might* have been mad, but there was no telling. They were all completely shrouded. 1660E1L11

It has been suggested that in this sentence the use of "have" constitutes an attempt to achieve correct treatment of tense-sequence.[7] (103c) is formally the past-modified version of both (103a) and (103b). If the writer wants a past-modified version of (103c), he adds another past modification in the only possible place, producing (103).

(103a) stands ... *may* be mad ... is no telling.
(103b) stands ... *might* be mad ... is no telling.
(103c) stood ... *might* be mad ... was no telling.
(103) stood ... *might* have been mad ... was no telling.

Aspect is used with *might* relatively frequently – six times. One of these appearances is a relatively complex verb phrase which shows phase modification in addition to aspect (104).

(104) "Seems to me last time I was here the grate bellowed out smoke as it *might* have been preparing us for hell". 0680E1K20

Phase is also used with passives, but not very frequently. The most complex of these verb phrases is (105), in which the "might have" is negated. This is, by the way, a good example of the effect that "not" has with *may/might* of negating only that portion of the verb phrase that follows the modal auxiliary. Speaking of negation, there are only three other cases of direct negation with *might*, of which none have a "not" negating the modal auxiliary. There are also four instances of indirect negation, all with "never".

(105) 3. The fact that AIA lists *might* not have been selected on a random basis. 1320E1J45

There is one sentence which sums up the essential difference between *can/could* and *may/might*. In sentence (106) *could* and *might* are both used in roughly parallel situations. Both receive contrary-to-fact meanings from the past tense and are put into time prior to that of the discourse of the text by the phase which accompanies them, so the difference must lie in the meanings of the modals themselves. Both are perfect examples of thier respective most typical meanings: *could* has the basic meaning, and *might* carries the balanced significance of *can* plus openness to occur-

[7] Again, my thanks to Mr. Francis.

rence. The fact that the writer did not choose to use *can* for both rather than for just one points up the fact of the extra meaning of *may*, while at the same time the parallel situation itself emphasizes that portion of meaning that the two modal auxiliaries have in common.

(106) . . . the still fragmentary local party organizations *could* have operated more effectively and parties *might* have been encouraged to state their positions more clearly. 1080E1J37

4. WILL

The meanings of *can*, *may*, and *will* seem to complement one another. From pure circumstance to combined circumstance and occurrence to pure occurrence one can move from one extreme to the other by means of a route from the fixed meaning of *can* through the flexible scale of *may* to the fixed meaning of *will*. The meaning of *will* differs from that of the occurrence dimension of *may* only by addition of positive factors; it may be phrased as "the occurrence of the predication is guaranteed". There are two overtones for this meaning, and, as in the case of *can*, they can both be seen as clearly participating in the basic meaning.

So far the behavior of *will* can be considered analogous to that of *can*. However, its pattern diverges from that of *can* on the important question of time. We saw that both *can* and *may* are time-neutral as far as the meaning of *nihil obstat* is concerned – context makes no difference in their time relations to the discourse surrounding them or to the utterances in which they appear, except for the fact that both have a past-tense form for sequence-of-tense past time and the rare cases of actual previous time reference. *Will*, on the other hand, is affected by its overall context so that it may either be time-neutral or represent a time future to that of the discourse, and *may*, to the extent that it displays the occurrence dimension, also has such time function. This factor of "time function" affects the basic meaning of *will* and both of the overtones.

Time function turns out to be clearly conditioned by the kind of context surrounding the verb phrase. When the context is one of general statement, usually of fact (107) or description (108) the auxiliary is time-neutral. No element of a unique sequence of predications is in evidence once a time-neutral *will* is stated; it is valid for any time. For instance, in sentence (107), the modal auxiliary says that the hypothetical example is such that its illustrating the point is assured. The use of the example would have illustrated the point if applied before the writing of the article, it is a fact that it does so illustrate, and finally it is assured of doing so at any time.

(107) A hypothetical example *will* illustrate this point. 1600E1J08
(108) . . . car loadings, while perhaps interesting enough, are not the magic formula that *will* always turn before stock prices turn. 0340E1J39

Neutral time function may be said to correspond to the contextually abstract. The other time function, future, may on the other hand be described in terms of an analogy with concreteness. It always occurs in contexts referring to specific situations, in which unique events follow a linear time-determined sequence. In this case, *will* can refer only to a single, specific, and unique predication, the occurrence of which is later than that of the discourse (109). Although specific sentence elements of several types can be used to clarify or specify the futurity in time (110), it frequently happens that no stated sentence elements can be found to force the future time reference (111).

(109) "Don't worry about it, Dave. Your acceptance *will* come through". 1090E1P27

(110) These findings, and others which *will* in time be developed, *will* affect the method of glottochronological inquiry. 1130E1J35

(111) You *will* get to come home on long weekends from Hanover, won't you? 0910E1L01

In the non-fictional texts most of the appearances of *will* are time-neutral by virtue of the generalized, often technical context in which they occur. However, in some cases even this type of text exhibits future time function. This seems to happen exclusively in three types of sentence, of which the first occurs when a writer establishes a usage or assumption which is to affect the remainder of his work (112). The futurity of this *will* is, of course, from the point of view of a writer in the process of writing and a reader in the process of reading.[1] In this case, as in the next, not only is the predication in time following that of the actual discourse, but the context itself moves from the generality of discussion of fact to the concreteness of the actual writing of the book. The second such case, then, is one in which a further activity involved in the writing or argument is mentioned (113). Finally, the last such future-time *will* is that which occurs in cases like (114), where actually existing, concrete situations are under discussion, so that again there is an event located in time which the modalized predication can follow.

(112) ... the corner not on the curve *will* be called the diagonal point of the square. 0300E1J20

(113) Other methods *will* be described below. 1360E1J09

(114) ... dealers plan to increase the mechanization of their materials handling in the coming two years. And most of the gain *will* be in self-unloading vehicles. 1310E1E35

Other than these somewhat special instances, future time appears most frequently in dialogue (dialogue accounts for 319 of the 652 occurrences of *will* including all 37 occurrences of *won't*, 91 of the 409 appearances of *will*, and 191 of the 206 uses of *'ll*). Indeed, all but a few of the occurrences in dialogue have future time function (109), (111). Those few which do not, include descriptions and two sentences in which the

[1] On the other hand, as W. N. Francis points out, from the point of view of actuality the whole book exists at the time of reading, which means a time-neutral interpretation.

modal could be interpreted either as future time or as time-neutral (115). A few occurrences in dialogue have a time-neutral *will* which appears in a general, abstract context within the dialogue (116).

(115) "Here, this *will* help", suggested Helva, . . . 0910E1M05

(116) They thought it would be a chance for you to make a life out where nobody *will* be thought any better than the next except for just what's inside of them. 0730E1N20

In a few dialogue examples a normal, descriptive time-neutral *will* appears with aspect modification. The effect of the added factor of limited duration in such cases is to make the entire verb phrase a statement of probability. While it retains the basic predictive meaning, *will* is contextualized in such a way that, for instance, sentence (117) says "you can probably find (or you can expect to find) Gyp holding forth in some bar. . ." rather than "Gyp has the habit of holding forth in some bar. . .". The second would be the proper paraphrase without the effect of pinning the action down to a single period of time which is added by aspect marking. This type of relatively rare effect constitutes the only case of a clearly present-tense reference for *will* as well as the only one in which probability is the primary effect of the time function (this is discussed further in the analysis of *would*). Otherwise, aspect as usual has no noticeable effect on the verb phrase.

(117) "Gyp'*ll* be holdin' forth in some bar if he's here at all", Cobb declared, . . . 0060E1N14

One interesting example (118) has two contiguous sentences, one of which is time-neutral, and one of which is time-future. Actually the first could also be interpreted as time-future, but if it is a descriptive time-neutral instance then it is enabled by a preceding time-neutral context established by the modal *can*, which we have already seen to be unaffected by time relations.

(118) "But you can't ride into the Ferry. That's what they'*ll* expect you to do. They'*ll* be there waiting for you. . ." 1180E1N07

Some grammarians refer to iterative or habitual action as meanings of *will*. What they refer to is the time-neutral *will* which appears in generalized contexts of description. Sentence (119) illustrates what might be called habitual action and (120) illustrates iterative action, though much of the notion of iteration is carried by the adverb "occasionally". Both illustrate the basic meaning appearing in contexts of description and statement of fact. The context then conditions the time function, as stated before.

(119) . . . [it] possesses only a large number of long, branched hairs on its legs, on which the pollen grains *will* collect. 1440E1J10

(120) . . . but sometimes a man in Miyagi or Akita prefectures is much more hairy

than the average Japanese, and occasionally a girl *will* be strikingly lovely, . . .
0120E1P05

Contrast between the ordinary present tense and time-neutral *will* results in an emphasis on the guaranteed (i.e. predictive) quality of *will.* In (121), if one substitutes the copula "is" for "will . . . be", as in (121a), the modal, contingent quality of *will* is pointed up (the contingency derives from the fact that it is the state of the environment which assures the occurrence). By making use of the modal to state that one can expect to find dominant stress on the predicator, the possibility that one might not is also implied (even if denied). With the simple copula such contingent complications do not enter the picture at all. Sentence (122) illustrates a similar situation where the two forms are actually contrasted. For such an interpretation, of course, *will* must be time-neutral (and *may* must show a balanced meaning). Otherwise *will* and the present tense of "suits" are primarily in time contrast if *will* is time-future (in which case *may* is occurrence-heavy).

(121) . . . in *one thing I know* [dominant stress] *will* usually be on the predicator *know*. 0220E1J33

(121a) . . . in *one thing I know* dominant stress is usually on the predicator *know*.

(122) This conflict may be resolved in a way which *will* suit white middle-class people better than it suits white lower-class people. 0330E1J49

So far all the examples discussed illustrate the basic meaning, with either time-neutral or time-future function. As stated before, however, *will* also has two overtones, each of which may appear with either time function.

The first of these is a relatively uncomplicated one which refers to a relation of cause-and-effect, as in (123), logical sequence, as in (124), or simply one event following another, as in (125). All of these are time-neutral, so needless to say in the case of sentence (125) both events, although in relation to one another they are sequential, must in relation to the discourse be time-neutral. That is to say, when such a sequence of verb phrases is time-neutral, it must be considered a single time-neutral unit, even though it may have a fairly rigid internal sequential structure.

(123) The smaller the particle the further it *will* travel downwind before settling out. 0550E1J08

(124) . . . such a man is indeed of an animal nature; and, being left carnal, he *will* be an imperfect being, . . . 0460E1D04

(125) . . . as historic processes of modernization gradually gain momentum, their cohesion *will* be threatened by divisive forces, the gaps between rulers and subjects, town and country, *will* widen; . . . 0030E1J22

This kind of overtone, in which *will* carries a sort of "if . . ., then . . ." force, appears also in future time function, but then the entire sequential unit must be later than the discourse. In (126) both acts are seen as happening after the concrete context of the dialogue in which they appear. In three sentences, exemplified by (127), the concrete context requires a future time function, but the predication of which the modalized verb phrase is a guaranteed consequent is present in time (concurrent with the time of the utterance). As a result, strictly speaking this sentence and those like it cannot be considered examples of the first (sequential) overtone. They must be seen as examples of the basic meaning instead, through which they illustrate the necessarily close connection between the basic use and this overtone.

(126) Perhaps if they know the story there *will* be a massive cry of indignation. 1290E1K17

(127) "All right, kid, if that's how you want it, that's how it'*ll* be." 0690E1P22

Example (128) shows that in this overtone the first act need not always be expressed; Fanny and Mrs. Godwin will be glad only after they have been told, so again the predication modified by *will* is dependent upon the occurrence of another act. A similar case for the neutral time function may be noted in (129), where an "after you follow these directions" must be inferred by the reader. This is also the case in what might be called "rhetorical address", as in (130). Here "after I told you" is implied.

(128) "Fanny and Mrs. Godwin *will* probably be glad to hear that Mary has safely recovered..." 1360E1K20

(129) You'*ll* have the neighbor's eyes popping as well as their mouths watering! 1200E1E14

(130) This, you *will* remember, was still New Year's [Eve] ... 0170E1L11

Will following imperatives carries the same overtone. Sentence (131) appears in a general context, so it is time-neutral, but such a use with time-future meaning in dialogue is easy to imagine. Unfortunately no such use actually appears in the sample, but it is frequent in speech.

(131) Pick the flowers, keep the soil dampened, and each of the pegged-down branches *will* take root and become a little plant and go on blooming for the rest of the season. 0820E1E02

The second overtone is volitional. This is not so clear-cut as the first; it permits a range of volitional force that begins with a touch of willingness in what would otherwise be the pure basic meaning, as in (132). The other extreme would include sentences like (133), where the volitional element almost takes on the force of a command. In all these gradations, however, the basic meaning never fades out to the same degree as one dimension or the other did in the case of *may*. Even in the extreme sentence (133) the predictive element is enhanced by the volitional element rather than overshadowed by it.

(132) "We *will both* go back, Laban!" 0110E1P03

(133) ... John's reply was always the same: "Anything that affects souls is the concern of the Church! We *will* have righteousness!" 1070E1K10

There are other reasons for considering this an overtone and not a separate dimension of meaning. First of all, volition and occurrence are closer to each other in content than are occurrence and circumstance. Volition may be described as deriving from prediction in that for *will* it is a case of the subject's acting as one of the guarantors of the occurrence of the predication. Like some of the cases of the first overtone (sequential, expressing cause and effect and logical constraint), then, volitional overtones specify the "something" which contributes to assuring occurrence.

This situation is especially clear in the case of first person singular uses of the modal auxiliary. Here not only does the subject of the verb phrase provide part of the guarantee, but since the subject and the speaker (or writer) are the same, two guaranteeing factors of the occurrence are specified instead of just one (134).

(134) Fat, hey? I taught him, dammit, and I'*ll* teach you. 0540E1K24

Not surprisingly, first person occurrences appear almost always in dialogue, and they account for more than half of the contracted occurrences of *will*. Of all of these, a considerable minority are first person plural. The modals with plural subject generally (but not always) carry less volitional force than the singular forms; this phenomenon may be seen in the case of (135), in which the first *will* is a very mildly volitional first person plural future-time instance, the second is a time-neutral example of basic meaning conditioned by the "any time", and the last is a first person singular future-time volitional in which the subject expresses slightly more than willingness by volunteering. The point of this example is that the "we will" is close to being a pure prediction like (136). However, in the latter the subject has nothing to do with guaranteeing the eating, while in the former (135) he does have some such role.

(135) ". . . We'*ll* have oystchers – couple bar'l oystchers'*ll* fetch in a crowd any time. I'*ll* see word gets round". 1580E1P03
(136) At least we'*ll* eat, I thought grimly as I put all the food away. 1510E1P18

We can now return to the second reason for the fact that volition is a subsidiary overtone of *will*, not a separate dimension of meaning. This is the fact that while prediction pervades all volitional occurrences in more or less constant force, no element of volition at all appears in the majority of the occurrences of *will*. To be sure, volition is present in considerably more of the dialogue uses than the non-dialogue uses, but it also constitutes less than two-thirds of the occurrences with the first person singular, where its use would show up most conspicuously.

Time function distinctions operate for this overtone as they did for the other; it is, however, of interest to note that while the sequential overtone occurred far more often with neutral time function, the volitional is a predominantly time-future overtone. Time-neutral volitional *will* occurs only twice (137), and both cases may as easily be interpreted as having only the basic meaning. It occurs not at all with *won't* and only once with '*ll* (138) – and again this could also be considered a descriptive basic meaning occurrence. This rarity comes as no surprise when one sees that for volition to occur in time-neutral context it would have to survive two derivational processes, out of the first of which developed prediction, and out of the second of which developed the time-function dichotomy which characterizes *will.*

(137) However, there always is some limit to the numbers who *will* spend the time and effort to acquire training. 1470E1J38

(138) I believe in returning favors. I'*ll* do anything for somebody I like. 0490E1L23

In a very few examples like (139) and (140) we can see something which looks very much like what would probably be called transitional forms in a diachronic description. The first appears in a Biblical quotation (but would be acceptable in a certain type of writing today), and both are limited to use in a rather nonspecific propredicate, a polite imperative in one case. It is interesting to note that filling the propredicate with the rest of a verb phrase weakens the volitional force to the degree where it simply adds willingness to what is otherwise simply a prediction. (140), of course, is an idiomatic fixed phrase.

(139) The wind blows where it *will,* and thou hearest its sound but dost not know where it comes from or where it goes... 1110E1D16

(140) ... and if you should be joined by – anybody – try to keep things quiet, if you *will.* 1130E1L02

Will appears in three different forms in this sample. The contracted form '*ll* occurs 191 times out of 206 in dialogue, as mentioned above. This results from a predominance of personal pronoun subjects in dialogue, most of which are, as was already discussed, first person singular. The majority have future time function for reasons also previously discussed (the kind of context provided by most of the dialogue), but about one eighth are time-neutral.

Much the same situation holds for *won't.* All the occurrences appear in dialogue, the majority of the subjects are personal pronouns (but "I" does not predominate as it did in the case of '*ll*), and all but one (141) have future time function. The basic meaning and both overtones occur; (142) illustrates the sequential overtone, (143) illustrates the basic meaning, and (144) serves as an example of volitional *won't.* The volitional element is particularly distinct in these negated cases. Such forms can then serve as a means of determining whether or not a positive *will* or '*ll* carries volitional overtones. If negation brings out a notion of refusal, then such a form may be classified as a volitional in its positive form as well.

(141) "I have a thousand things for you to do. Doors that *won't* open, and doors that *won't* close and shelves and broken ..." 1590E1R04

(142) If we let them go, they *won't* stay away, they'*ll* find men to ride with them and they'*ll* be back. 1260E1N02

(143) "See for yourself, Miss Zion. It *won't* take a minute." 1720E1P03
(144) "I have talked to him, but you know I've never tried to push him into any profession. I *won't* be guilty of trying to run his life." 1670E1P27

This and other forms of negation (direct and indirect) may be translated as "something guarantees that the predication does *not* occur" or "there is a guarantee against the occurrence of the action". This means that even in the contracted form *won't* the negation applies to what follows the modal rather than to the modal itself. In (145) the non-use of the contraction *won't* emphasizes the fact that "not" modifies the predicate as far as the predictive meaning of *will* is concerned.

(145) "Very well", she said, "I'*ll* not catechize you." 0960E1K20

The existence of this contrasting form makes it necessary to try to find a reason conditioning its use. It turns out that while negation never refers to the basic predictive elements of *will*, in occurrences of *won't* it does negate the volitional elements of the modal auxiliary when they are present. The contrast between the behavior of the predictive and the volitional in *won't* and *will/'ll not*, then, is probably a further reflection of the original meaning structure of *will*. Here we can do no more than speculate, but it seems likely that if for a specific modal the normal pattern of negation for modal auxiliaries applies only to an overtone, this could well be because the overtone was the original modal meaning.

There is one special use worth noting. There seems to be a one-to-one correlation between volitional overtone and interrogation, which gives an imperative force to the verb phrase in (146). Not only does this use appear in direct questions, but it also occurs in all tag-question occurrences of volitional *will* following actual imperatives (147). Such an example definitely points up the imperative force of this use. Although it has been stated above that this is interrogative, there is one case (148) where the interrogation has become a truly imperative exclamation; but the inversion is retained, so the determining factor is probably inversion rather than interrogation as such. This conclusion is supported by the fact that interrogations with other overtones show no particular effects. In the two occurrences of this use with *won't* the effect of negation seems to be to add a polite element that would ordinarily be added by the past tense by emphasizing the volitional element through use of the negative (149).

(146) "I am not pulling your leg. *Will* you call that captain?" 0180E1L16
(147) "Make it as snappy as you can, *will* you?" 0450E1L02
(148) ". . . Hey, *will* you look at that?" 0900E1P16
(149) ". . . *Won't* you step into the living room, where it's cozier?" 0940E1K22

There is an interesting carryover in the case of time-neutral basic meaning *will* when used with the personal pronoun "you" (150). This is because the first and second person pronouns are used almost exclusively in dialogue, which as we have seen usually has a time-future function because of its concrete context. As a result, use of the generalized unstressed "you" produces a stronger feeling of concrete context and time-future function than would the equivalent non-personal "one". Sentence (150a) provides a comparison.

(150) You *will* find that avocado is unlike any other fruit you have ever tasted. 1160E1E02

(150a) One *will* find that avocado is unlike any other fruit he has ever tasted.

As we have seen, aspect usually does not have any effect with *will*, but it sometimes can. Passive modification seems to do nothing to the verb phrase. Phase occurs only once (151), and its effect includes the usual perfectivization and current relevance to a future time. It puts the predication into a time earlier than that of the modal but not of the discourse itself.

(151) ". . . Hell, in a year or five or ten, the boy *will* have forgotten me – his own father!" 0630E1N10

WOULD

The behavior of the past tense with *will* is not altogether like its behavior with *can* and *may*. Because part of the meaning of *will* is dependent upon a context-determined time function, the addition of a past-tense factor must be seen as an addition to the context. As a result, not only may it cause the addition to the predictive basic meaning of *will* of the elements of past time, sequence of tense, and non-actuality, but these factors may have a further effect on the element of time function that we saw running through all the occurrences of the present-tense form.

Sequence of tense is probably the most common reason for use of past modification. Under circumstances requiring sequence-of-tense past, time function is undisturbed; all the overtones previously discussed for *will* appear with *would* when it is forced by a preceding verb in the past. Thus the basic meaning appears in both time functions, as in (152), which illustrates the neutral time function, and (153), in which we can see the future time function. Here the past tense has no effect on the meaning, nor has it in a case like (154), in which the past tense verb that forces the past modal also helps to condition the future time function. Similarly, verbs of hoping or speaking can contribute to the requirement of a time-future modal, as in (155).

(152) . . . but he soon saw, as did she, that this course if persisted in *would* involve them in a common ruin. 1700E1K20

(153) Martha presumably *would* cope. She might be firm. It was most unlikely that she *would* be firm. 1510E1L14

(154) But one day, she expected, he *would* somehow discover, without her having to tell him, that there was such a woman in the world; . . . 1400E1L10

(155) She promised that she *would* soon take a few day's leave and visit the uncle she had never seen, . . . 1240E1P05

We can note in passing that sentence (153) also serves to illustrate the difference between the expression of occurrence in *may/might* and in *will/would.* The contrast between the negative "the non-occurrence of the predication is not guaranteed" and "the occurrence of the predication is guaranteed" is unmistakeable and even emphasized by the proximity of the two modals. Another contrast emphasizes the future time function of *will* (again in a concrete context) that has resulted in its being referred to as the "future tense" (156).

(156) ... but that was where everyone was, or *would* be. 0350E1K26

In some cases, neutral time function is also conditioned, so that in (157) the "always" in the sense of "in any case" makes a generalized, "as-a-rule" context unmistakeable. On the other hand, use of a lexical stem that usually implies a time span between utterance and predication does not necessarily mean that the modal must assume future time function (158), and even in a concrete overall context, a general context restricted to the sentence in which the modal occurs will result in neutral time function, as in the case of (159). More context than this is usually required to determine the time function of the modal auxiliary; thus, (160) may be interpreted as having either time function as long as more context is not added.

(157) ... he told Boats McCafferty that Hong Kong was a book he had read before, and the Navy *would* always bring him there again, some day. 1580E1P05
(158) ... one of those things one does say, lightly, meaning nothing. Which probably *would* turn out to be true; ... 1240E1L14
(159) With a cop patrolling the road Muller *would* have to be inside a building – 1090E1L16
(160) Promptly at seven he *would* clatter out of the court with twelve in the tallyho. 1060E1E11

Interestingly enough, the time-neutral use of the modal auxiliary in (161) requires that the word "prophecy" be interpreted to mean "prediction" in the sense that it has been used here in reference to *will*, that is, as a statement of guaranteed occurrence of the predication without automatic reference to time relationship.

(161) ... Parker vindicated Channing's further prophecy that he who committed this infraction of taste *would* promptly discover how little mercy liberals were disposed to allow ... 1300E1D05

What was previously called the sequential overtone, the one in which the *will* expresses a logical, causal, or sequential relation between one action or fact and another, also appears to be unaffected by sequence of tenses in the rather few cases in which *would* occurs simply as a sequence-of-tense form. As before it is usually indicated by stated elements of the sentence in which it occurs. The same is true for "if"-clauses which are also past because of sequence of tense. The sequential overtone generally means that the guarantor of the occurrence is explicit, but again, as before, it need not be expressed. In (162) the factors which require the waiting could be expressed, but instead they are taken for granted. Similarly in (163) the unexpressed guaranteeing factor includes Hope's implied authority to decree that nobody will have the heater.

(162) Linda *would* have to wait, she knew. 1250E1P17
(163) . . . but Hope said if Grandma *wouldn't* have the heater nobody *would* have it, so Grandma had to give in. 1710E1P02

All of the preceding examples had neutral time function. With sequence-of-tense *would* and *wouldn't*, future time function in this overtone is infrequent, but in (164) there is a multiple predicate with a single initiating factor (backing against the fence) in a concrete, unique-sequence-of-events context. There are no examples of this overtone with an implied cause or guarantor for future time function as there was for neutral time (162).

(164) If he backed against the fence, one of the cars *would* brush him as it passed, and he *would* be cruelly lacerated by the wire. 1300E1L04

In cases of contracted -'*d* the situation is the reverse of the statistical situation for the full forms because of the larger proportion of dialogue uses. Dialogue generally indicates a concrete situation, in which the time function is future. All but one of the sequential instances of contracted *would* have future time function; (165) is a good example of this. The only exception (166) does not appear in a specific, concrete context.

(165) But he'*d* find out about this one because we were using it. 1330E1K24
(166) . . . she played a little game with herself, seeing how downright rude she could act to the others, before they'*d* take offense, threaten to call the manager. 1090E1L08

The last overtone appearing with *will* was the volitional. We have seen that this overtone, regardless of time function, can appear in varying degrees of strength ranging from willingness to insistence. As long as past tense of the modal results from sequence of tense only, this situation remains undisturbed. Some examples of time-neutral volitional *would* include (167), (168), (169), (170), and possibly (171). Item (167) may be interpreted either as willingness or as a stronger form of volition approaching desire. If the second is the case, then this is the closest the corpus comes to the pure sequence-of-tense past of volitional *will* if it is not negated. If used in speech such a use of *would* would have a distinctly archaic sound to the present-day listener unless provided with emphatic stress.

(167) The only one who *would* have him was his cripple, the strange unhappy woman who became his wife. 1030E1K03
(168) But now he was happy she *would* let him straighten out her life and take care of her. 1560E1P08

(169) Red man or white man, pacifist or killer, the forest *would* accept them all – 0870E1N08

(170) I went off with Cousin Simmons, who maintained that if he didn't see to me, he didn't know who *would.* 1440E1K09

(171) . . . there would always be transient young men who *would* approach her with broken English. 1040E1P05

As in the case of *will*, negation, both direct and indirect, makes the volitional element clearer. Indeed, in (172) the volitional element is actually one of determination rather than the willingness in varying degrees that characterizes the rest of the examples given so far. Sentence (173) expresses recalcitrance of non-animate subjects and will be discussed in more detail later.

(172) He *would* never let her harm herself again. 1570E1P08

(173) At the rear of the auditorium, upstairs, some men tried to push open the door to the box corridor. It *would* not give. 1540E1K05

There is one sentence of some interest because of the use of the qualifying adverb "voluntarily" (174). The adverb has the function of relieving any possible ambiguity between the basic meaning and the volitional element, but it is of interest just because it emphasizes how volition has ceased to occupy central position in the range of meaning of *will/would* and has reached the point where it is compatible with adverbial reinforcement.

(174) The cops would gather up Connor and the foursome on the third floor and bring us those of them who *would* voluntarily submit to fingerprinting. 1370E1L11

In (175) there is a kind of dual volitional element. The effect of the lexical item "have" heavily overshadows the volitional element in *would*, but it can nevertheless be interpreted as expressive of a mild willingness that serves as an overtone to the ever-present predictive element. In (163) there is a good illustration of the contrast between the volitional and sequential overtones, but the element common to both, the basic meaning, is discernible.

(175) "Who do you think pays the rent? You *wouldn't* have me throw the poor boy out on the street", 0870E1K18

Future-time volitionals show the same sort of variations in strength of the volitional element as do the neutral-time forms, and negation again reinforces the volitive meaning (176). Future-time volitionals are considerably more frequent than their neutral-time counterparts, and, although expression of willingness does occur, ex-expression of intention, understandably, appears in greater proportion for future time. Worth special mention is (177), in which the propredicate repetition of the initial contracted modal provides an emphasis to substitute for the stress the contraction cannot bear. This way the writer may be said to have his cake (the stylistic effect of the contraction) and eat it too (emphasis on the volitional modal).

(176) Despite his yearning, the colonel *would* not go down to see the men come through the lines. He *would* remain in the tent, waiting impatiently, occupied by some trivial task. 0050E1K21

(177) He'*d* come East for the Christening, by God he *would.* 1480E1K18

(178) is volitional and particularly archaic, which seems incompatible with the style of the surrounding horse-opera narrative. The affirmative use of volitional *would* is rare.

(178) Cabot turned back to the men and he was drunk with the thing they *would* do, . . . 1320E1N02

There are two uses of *will* which appear in this sample more clearly with sequence-of-tense past than they did with the present tense form. The first is a descriptive use. In the present tense, the closest that any of the sentences in this sample came to it was the unsatisfactory (119). Since all that can be said about such present-tense descriptive sentences is that they are time-neutral and therefore may refer to any time relative to that of the discourse (and may therefore be interpreted as future as easily as present), the reader cannot be certain that they consist solely of what I am calling "descriptive" *will.* In the case of the past tense, however, there is seldom any such doubt, and when there is, further context will generally serve to resolve it.

Descriptive *would* is necessarily limited to the time preceding the utterance since it indicates that the action has ceased before the time of the utterance. As a result, it cannot, strictly speaking, be considered a neutral-time occurrence. Since it does not occur in specific, concrete contexts, it is not time-future. In the present tense (179a), it refers to a prediction based on past observation of iterative or habitual action which is unaffected by time function; it acts in much the same way as a general rule does. In the past (179) it retains the general, non-concrete context but acquires a previously nonexistent time relation to the time of the utterance as described above. It therefore is made past both by sequence of tense and by actual past-time reference, even when used in a form of indirect discourse in which one would expect sequence of tense to be the only reason for its being in the past. It also retains neutral time function. However, in the only example in this sample of indirect discourse and descriptive *would* (180), we can see again that it, too, refers to past time and that, furthermore, additional context is necessary to determine whether or not the modal is descriptive or a time future volitional.

(179) . . . and when she gardened she *would* eat dinner with dirt on her calves. 0900E1K25

(179a) . . . and when(ever) she gardens, she *will* eat dinner with dirt on her calves.

(180) . . . and an old buddy of his told me he *would* come down on Sundays to the Pentagon and read the citations for medals— 0730E1K03

There seems to be some sort of correlation between the effect of the past tense and the type of meaning, except, perhaps, when an indirect discourse construction actually conditions strictly sequence-of-tense effect and the consequent ambiguity mentioned above. This can be considered an overtone in its own right, except for the fact that it differs from those already described in that it appears only with neutral time function, since it actually requires a general context because of its meaning. That is, habitual or iterative action cannot possibly be a part of a single, unique sequence of events. It can be considered an overtone because it is a clear derivative of the basic meaning, but it requires a considerable and indeterminable quantity of context to distinguish it from the basic meaning and other more easily identified overtones (adverbs and adverbial phrases are, of course, quite helpful; in (181) they eliminate any possibility of interpreting this sentence as a basic meaning with future time function).

(181) The State cops *would* check from time to time; pass word when there was word to pass. 0710E1L14

Because the different overtones may be conditioned by different contextual factors, and because these factors may occur simultaneously, it is not surprising to find that descriptive *will* appears with the time-neutral variants of the sequential (182) and volitional (183) overtones. In (184) the interpretation may be either descriptive or a combination of expressed-cause sequential and volitional. If it is descriptive, it may be paraphrased to read "Their demand . . . could never have been interpreted to mean that they generally followed . . ."

(182) . . . the powerful microphone I could press against the wall between my motel unit and that occupied by the man *would* bring in the sound of any conversation, . . . 1350E1L02

(183) He was six feet one like his father, with big hands and a hairy chest, a man the weak and persecuted *would* turn to. 0220E1P16

(184) Their demand against the Calvinist Orthodoxy for intellectual liberty had never meant that they *would* follow "free inquiry" to the extreme of proclaiming Christianity a "natural" religion . . . 0240E1D05

There is another group of sentences in which there is some ambiguity about whether or not the *would* is descriptive or whether it has the basic meaning of *will*. What is interesting about sentence (173) is that if it is not seen as descriptive then it seems to carry an additional overtone of weak volition. Such sentences occur only with negation, so this may be partly an effect of the negator, which we have already seen to clarify the volitional element in other cases, but not entirely. The problem is that all these sentences also have inanimate subjects, causing volition to seem somewhat out of place. Somehow these would seem to mean some degree of personification of these subjects. This is the recalcitrant inanimate to which previous reference was made.

The second of the two new uses mentioned above, which does not seem to appear at all in present-tense *will*, is a rarer one expressing high probability[2] (185). With one exception (186) all the occurrences also appear with aspect modification of the verb as well, but it cannot be said that aspect alone conditions this type of *will*, for there are several occurrences of aspect where this peculiar use does not appear (187). However, these last few cases appear with a modal that has future time function, whereas all the probability uses would have neutral time function. Thus one can say that this use is indeed conditioned, but by two factors. The combination of these two factors also contributes to the fairly narrow limitation of this use to the time of the discourse, so again, strictly speaking, this might not be considered a neutral time use at all.

(185) – all over the city, at this hour, housewives *would* be fussing over stoves. 1370E1L16

(186) This *would* be Mahzeer's office. 0910E1L16

(187) And here all the time you knew the Sioux *would* be using our rifles on them! 0150E1N04

At the beginning of this section it was stated that the past tense, by constituting an additional context factor, has an effect on the time-function of *will*. We have seen that this is not really the case when past tense is a result of sequence-of-tense rules and therefore may bear some relation to the notion of past time. However, the non-actual past is a very important determiner of time function. In all but a very few (fewer than ten) cases, the modal has a neutral time function when the past tense is non-actual (188).

(188) Here, an apportionment, say, of $5,000,000 of the total costs to residential service as a class *would* include an allowance of perhaps 6 per cent . . . 0980E1J50

The reason for this is the nature of the non-actual past. If a predication is made hypothetical either by a conditional statement or by a contrary-to-fact hypothesis, then no matter how concrete the rest of its surrounding context is, those portions of the sentence centering around a verb in the non-actual past are part of a general context which does not reflect a unique sequence of events and which has therefore a neutral time function. Sentence (189) shows this. The verbal carries volitional overtones of willingness, and if *will* remained in the present, it would probably have future time function. However, the past tense makes the cardinal's approving a conditional possibility which is contingent on the further hypothesis that someone *might* ask or the issue *might* arise. It is thus removed from the main stream of events in the narrative and dialogue and put into a separate and unrelated time stream of its own. Its relation to the time of the rest of the discourse is one of neutrality.

(189) "I am working for the Cardinal of San Dionigi. I'm sure he *would* approve." 0840E1K14

[2] W. N. Francis comments that this often appears in a type of rather affected colloquial speech.

The same situation is illustrated by the ambiguous sentence (190), in which, it is interesting to note, a present-tense modal like *can* or *will* must be added to produce a sentence like (190a). If the auxiliary added is *will*, it is time-neutral and so is the following one (the conditioning factor here is the "if"-clause).

(190) She did not pause to consider what she *would* do if her plan should fail; . . .
0750E1N08

(190a) She *will* not pause to consider what she *will* do if her plan should fail.

Of the eight non-actual sentences where it seems difficult to insist on a neutral time function, four have the verb phrase containing *would* following "could wish" or "wished" (191). Even here, however, this can be considered a time-neutral use forced by the non-actual, hypothetical past, despite the fact that the action can only take place after the wishing. Although the major portion of the context would support a future time function, the most immediate context – and after all one could hardly ask for a more immediate contextual factor than a modification of the verb itself – seems to overrule. Even though the preterite form of the modals that have it is required by "wish", the very strong hypothetical notion of *would* is not lost; indeed, if anything it is easier to see.

(191) For once Cady Partlow wished Anne *would* yell at him so he could yell back.
1650E1P27

For the most part, the non-actual past of *will* is either very strongly conditional or it is contrary-to-fact. For a great many cases where the non-actual is not contrary to fact some sort of condition can be inferred, so that the most frequent total meaning of non-actual *would* is one of very contingent prediction. Thus in (192) there is an implied condition "if it were made". In some cases the contingency may be expressed; this is usually done by means of an "if"-clause but frequently some other way of expressing the contingency is found (193).

(192) Needless to say, any such inference *would* be quite unwarranted. 1280E1J50

(193) . . . but in this guileless manner he *would* probably receive more truthful answers than if he tried to get them by indirection. 0460E1K19

When the contingency is in an "if"-clause or other condition, there is a special kind of sequence-of-tense effect in operation. Sentence (194) serves as a good example. The past tense form of *would* is clearly forced by the preceding past of "did", but what is interesting about this type of conditional is that it, too, is carried by the sequence of tense. Thus, if the type of non-actuality (or even the whole idea of non-actuality itself) is really a property only of the verb phrase forcing the sequence-of-tense effect, one could say that the consequent *would* of which the condition is an antecedent has no such non-actual implication without the prior effect of the non-actual part of the condition. Such a condition may be expressed, as in the case of (194), where it is entirely hypothetical, or implied, as in the case of (192). Sentence (194) and its kind provide further evidence for the earlier statement that the two primary non-actual meanings are contrary to fact and hypothesis, not condition, which is subordinate to the other two and merely a particular kind of sequence of tense. Contrary-to-fact sentences behave in the same way as hypothetical ones.

(194) For if it did, the plane of *L* and *L'* *would* contain two generators of [**F][3] which is impossible. 0220E1J21

A result of this sequence-of-tense analysis of the conditional is that the "if"-clause can also be the preliminary element in the sequential overtone, where *will* expresses a relation somewhat like material implication. We have seen that the relation expressed by *will/would* is such that the preliminary statement in the sequence is enough to make a prediction of the consequent containing *will/would* a valid one (but the first statement need not be the only such guarantor). If, as in the case of (195), the "if"-clause proves to be a pure hypothesis, the whole thing can still act as a sequential set of verb phrases, in which farming out guarantees confusion. This sentence is of further interest in that there is yet another sequential relation implied. Confusion guarantees nervous breakdowns. It is valid to argue, then, that from this we can conclude that farming out guarantees nervous breakdowns (hypothetical syllogism).

(195) . . . if you tried to farm them out for two or three days every week they *would* become so confused that they *would* have nervous breakdowns. 0250E1R04

Needless to say, not all sentences containing non-actual "if"-clauses necessarily have sequential *will*, but, on the other hand, this is exactly what present-tense conditionals consist of. (The term "conditional" will continue to be used, for it is a convenient label for the effect of an expressed or expressible contingency.)

Would almost never occurs in the "if"-clause. There was one sentence in which an alternative interpretation of *would* could result in its being considered a non-actual past (196). In this case it would be of a volitional nature, though it is not an ordinary volitional but instead closer to the almost obsolete purely volitional *would* mentioned above. If this is the case, the following switch of tense would be more easily explainable, since *would* is a hypothetical preterite and therefore unaffected by ordinary sequence of tense.

(196) He took several large swallows, recollected that Docherty had gone up another flight, and decided he *would* be wise to cover himself by finding him. 0460E1L16

More ordinary time-neutral volitionals also appear with the non-actual past. The weakest and most frequent type of volition is willingness. There is a volitional of intention in (197) which would be considerably stronger than that of willingness if

[3] The bracketed symbols are used to indicate a formula or diagram which could not be included in the text.

there were not so noticeable an element of the basic predictive meaning as well, which results in a weakening of the volitional element.

(197) Let Old Knife come up and kill you and your people, or *would* you steer him on someone else?" 0200E1N04

The ambiguous sentence (198) serves two functions. First it demonstrates that the subdivisions which have been assumed for the volitional overtone are likewise context-conditioned, since more context is needed to determine whether the modal expresses willingness or the stronger notion of desire. It is interesting to speculate that these three subdivisions, willingness, desire, and intention, were originally the overtones of *will* when volition was its basic meaning, and part of the reason for their being retained after the major meaning shift is at least in part that the shift is not yet complete. The second function of this sentence is to introduce the element of desire, a stronger form of volition, which is also represented in sentence (199).

(198) At the same time, it was unlikely that any businessmen *would* spend a day in a Christian mission out of mere curiosity. 1050E1K19

(199) She couldn't see any reason why Maude *would* attempt to frighten her. 1200E1L09

Both of these last two examples show signs of similarity to the old use of purely volitional *would* in independent clauses which has been mentioned before. There are only two unambiguous occurrences of the purely volitional type of *would* in independent clauses. The first is so out of place to the modern eye except in the frame "as . . . *will/would* have it" that it must be classed as idiomatic (200). Even here, of course, there is enough of the predictive element that one can see how the present basic meaning was introduced. The second appears in a subordinate clause.

(200) . . . projecting from beneath the couch were a pair of feet which, as fate *would* have it, belonged to District Attorney Welch. 1220E1R01

Since this type of *would* has now become obsolete, the language of this sample has developed other ways to express the same notions of volition and deferent hypothesis. We have already discussed the first, which is that of the volitional overtone itself, but this adds, as we have seen, some element of the basic meaning at all times. The other way is more limited to the elements expressed by the older volitional *would.* It involves the combination of a strongly deferential and hypothetical *would* with a verb, usually a catenative, such as "like", "want" (201), "wish", or "be willing", or "mind". The primary function of *would* in such cases is to act as a carrier of the meaning of the non-actual past, so that the time-neutral, basic meaning of *will* often becomes very obscure – almost non-existent.

(201) "I *would* not want my people to get in trouble with the Church." 0820E1K14

In the case of "would rather" the old volitional again survives but has become so closely related to "rather" that the whole thing seems to be an idiomatic phrase in which "rather" is a verb like the five listed above and *would* is again a deferential non-actual basic. This certainly seems to be the case in (202), but in (203) the real situation is clear because of the peculiar structure of the whole relative clause.

(202) She *would* rather live in danger than die of loneliness and boredom. 1180E1K22
(203) . . . which she *would* die rather than acknowledge to her husband, . . .
0950E1P03

Sentence (204) shows how the context has its effect on the overtone of the modal. Here the conditioning factor is most explicit, for it is in the lexical verbs following the two modals, which themselves have the basic meaning and the weak volitional overtone respectively. Unfortunately the conditioning factors are usually not so explicit and situations of such convenient contrast seldom occur.

(204) . . . even if a sound could take shape within her parched mouth, who *would* hear, who *would* listen? 1630E1N08

There are two non-actual cases of the use discussed above [page 66, items (185) and (186)] which expresses probability. The first, (205), is probably an ordinary conditional with an unexpressed "if"-clause, and the second, (206), is probably a polite and deferential hypothetical example.

(205) He had no idea where Seward's room *would* be. 0190E1K05
(206) That *would* be Minerva, I suppose. 0860E1K20

As was the case for the other modal auxiliaries with past-tense forms, it frequently happens that the hypothetical meaning of the auxiliary is not dependent on a sequence of tense relation deriving from an "if"-clause but rather that the modal itself is expressive of non-actuality in its own right. This is well exemplified in (207), where the hypothetical nature of the modal is emphasized by the statement "it is our hypothesis". This type of independent hypothesis also occurs in conjunction with "seem" and "expect" (208) and operates by focussing attention on the contingency of the predication rather than the guarantee. "Would expect" occurs frequently in the passive; both are used primarily in technical articles and thus appears to be a form of hedging particularly frequent in academic style.

(207) . . . it is our hypothesis that all such conditions *would* have as a common factor the capacity to induce an attitude. . . 1050E1J28
(208) These are fluids which one *would* expect to be less viscoelastic or more Newtonian because of their lower molecular weight. 0410E1J03

The use of an "independent" hypothetical past accounts for the situation in (209). At first glance this sentence seems to contradict earlier statements about the nature of the conditional. However, there is really no problem, since the if-then relation can be interpreted as the sequential overtone of a time-neutral, present-tense *will* which becomes past either because of a separate, unstated "if"-clause or because of the independent hypothetical effect of the past. Because it is difficult to find an additional hypothetical past-tense "if"-clause to fit this sentence comfortably, the second interpretation here seems to be the better of the two alternatives.

(209) However, if Federal funds are used, it *would* be entirely appropriate to train workers for jobs which could be obtained elsewhere... 1670E1J38

The non-actual past tense meaning probably never completely takes over the entire modal, but sometimes it comes quite close to doing so. We have seen that it can do this in the cases of *would* after expressions of wish and preceding certain lexical items, usually catenative verbs (*wish*, *want*, *be willing*, *seem*, *mind*, *expect*, *prefer*, *rather*, and, in one case, *hate*). The polite use of the hypothetical past also seems to be limited primarily to these items and to a certain degree to the time-neutral probability use (206). There are a few conditional polite uses, such as (210), in which the polite predication is a parenthetical phrase bearing the unexpressed contingency "if you were to ask me".

(210) "Mr. Hohlbein and I have noticed some lapses since, though. Most of them this past year, I'*d* say . . ." 0890E1L15

Sentence (193) is a good example of the sort of ambiguity which can occur with a non-actual past. That is, there is room for doubt in such a sentence as to whether or not the predication is past in relation to the time of the utterance or whether it is concurrent with it. If there is such an element of past time, the past tense of the modal ceases to carry non-actual force, though the basic meaning of the verbal itself remains unchanged. Such ambiguity is handled in the English of this sample by the use of phase modification of the lexical verb. When phase has this function of relieving ambiguity it behaves just as it did for *can/could* and *may/might*. That is, the meanings of the past tense and of *will* remain unchanged, but the whole predication is put into a time prior to that of the utterance itself or that of the discourse within the utterance. Sentence (211) illustrates this point. The fact, by the way, that the "if"-clause is not also in the "pluperfect" emphasizes the fact that it refers primarily to the past-tense modal and not really to the entire verb phrase.

(211) The way MacArthur said his line – if you had the recorded transcript of a professional linguist – *would* probably have gone like this: 0110E1F01

Sometimes perfectivization is a more active factor in the relief of ambiguity than the past time relation established by the modification. This certainly seems to be the case in (212), though it must be noted that the time relation is not omitted.

(212) One night, so some of these theories run, Adam *would* have fallen asleep, much as he fell asleep for the creation of Eve; and thus he *would* have been carried over into the life eternal. 1480E1D04

Infrequently there is a particular action which the ambiguity-relieving "have" precedes: thus, in (213) if it reads like (213a), it is not clear whether or not this is a time-neutral basic meaning affected by ordinary sequence of tense or whether it is the same thing but with a non-actual past. The "have" forces the verb phrase to a time prior to the beginning of the statue and thus leaves it clear that the past tense of the modal is non-actual.

(213) . . . too careful or detailed studies in clay and wax *would* have glued him down to a mere enlarging of his model. 1360E1K14

(213a) . . . too careful or detailed studies in clay and wax *would* glue him down to a mere enlarging of the model.

There are three cases of a double use of phase where ordinarily one would expect but one (214). Analysis of these shows that the effect of the first "have" in all three is to establish the time-relation; the second seems to do most of the perfectivizing. Thus in (214) the first "would have" puts the predication before the thought comes, and the second refers to a specific and single action.

(214) . . . it comes to you that maybe it *would* have been better to have made somebody else happy if you couldn't be happy yourself. 0990E1P09

The remaining major overtone, the sequential one, also appears with phase. It is interesting to note that the non-actual past is in this case always a contrary-to-fact conditional, so that, as before, the place where the meaning of the non-actual past of *would* is determined is the "if"-clause that may also serve as the antecedent of the sequential *will.* If the antecedent contingency is contrary to fact, then what follows from it is also contrary to fact. (On the other hand, a contrary-to-fact past tense does not always require a sequential overtone for *would* any more than any non-actual modal has to be a conditional). Furthermore, if a hypothetical statement is clearly prior to the time of utterance or of the discourse, its truth-value is likely to be more apparent than that of one which has no place in the time sequence in question. This accounts for the fact that a great many of the examples of non-actual modal plus phase carry some degree of contrary-to-fact significance, while in sentences without phase, this special type of hypothesis is rare.

Negation for *would* behaves much as it did with *will.* When it occurs with a volitional modal (215) it generally refers to the auxiliary; otherwise it refers to the remainder of the predication (216), except when contracted (217). It is curious, by the way, that for some reason only about half the contracted negated occurrences of *would* appear in dialogue, as do fewer than half of the cocurrences of contracted *would* (most of the remaining occurrences are in informal fictional narrative).

(215) Curt was in almost as bad shape, but he *wouldn't* quit. 1470E1N12

(216) Indian ghosts *would* not impinge upon his nights. . . 0950E1N08

(217) He hoped he *wouldn't* be forced to use it in taking care of the Beach detectives, but its weight was comforting at his hip. 1270E1L05

Since the first person singular pronoun is sometimes a cause of argument when it is used with *will,* I have counted that with *will* "I" is used 112 times out of a total of 653, of which 59 were volitional. With *would* it appears 45 times out of a total of 1,038 occurrences. Of these, only 7 are volitional.

5. SHALL

Shall occurs thirty times in this corpus. Of these, nine, or nearly a third, are in quotations from considerably older sources, principally the Bible. It is interesting that these nine quotations account for all cases of a use of *shall* with a subject other than a first-person personal pronoun (218). Thus all other contemporary uses have "I" or "we" as subject, so that it may be said of the present-day usage, at least of this sample, that *shall* is most likely to be a stylistic device expressing the same basic meaning as that of *will* but also reflecting a quantity of formal education which the writer wants to show.

(218) "*What shall it profit a man, if he shall gain the whole world* (that includes outer space), *and lose his own soul*? . . . 1351E1D06

This may explain the fact that eleven of the remaining sentences appear in technical, particularly mathematical, articles and have the editorial "we" as subject (219). Among other functions of the editorial "we", it carries indications of a certain level of literacy. In a sentence like (220), however, the *shall* which the writer has used seems to have been forced for him by his editorial "we" (this is supported by the use of *will* in the same sentence but with a noun subject). The co-occurrence of the two modals in the one sentence further shows that both modals have the same meaning, which is time-neutral sequential. However, the use of *shall*, even as a stylistic device occurring with a first-person subject, is quite inappropriate in this sentence, for the editorial "we" is really an impersonal bearing almost nothing of a first-person significance, which means that this sentence could be seen as almost equivalent to "one shall have". Perhaps it can be considered an example of a type of hyperurbanism.

(219) . . . then we *shall* show that the space *V* is the direct sum of the null spaces of **F. 0270E1J18

(220) When **F for each *I*, we *shall* have **F, because the operator **F *will* then be 0 on the range of **F. 0850E1J18

For the most part the meaning of *shall* is identical with the predictive basic meaning of *will* (221). Sentence (222) carries a certain feeling of intention, but this is the closest that *shall* comes to expressing any form of volition. The sequential overtone also appears. The absence of volitional overtone, of course, is because of an earlier split in which *shall* was predictive or compulsive and *will* was more strictly volitional.[1] With the change in the meaning of *will*, predictive *shall* developed no new meaning and so was supplanted in ordinary use by *will*, except for a limited appearance with the first person, which, as has already been mentioned, resulted in its becoming a stylistic substitute for *will* indicating sufficient education to have been exposed to prescriptive grammar. It is, therefore, not surprising that volition plays almost no part in the meaning of *shall*, except for the expectable amount which results from the fact that the speaker is guaranteeing the occurrence of his own act.

(221) There we *shall* be free and unknown; 0190E1K20

(222) For the reason just suggested, I *shall* assume the use of the first subtype of fully distributed cost apportionment in the following simplified example. 1290E1J50

The small amount of meaning which is independent of most instances of *will* involves the fact that if speaker and subject are one and the same, the speaker can often constitute another guaranteeing factor. Even this, as we saw in the discussion of *will*, is not really independent for first-person subjects, because many of the first-person instances of *will* also carry the notion of subject-speaker guarantee. It is this portion of the meaning of *shall*, however, resulting from its almost exclusive use with "I" and "we", which accounts for its frequent use with second- and third-person subjects in decrees or certain types of officialese. In such cases, of which there are no examples in this corpus, the subject's role in the assurance is lost, and what persists is the writer's or speaker's function as a guarantor of the prediction. Thus such a *shall* can mean "the predication is guaranteed because I say so." Such a "compulsive" *shall* also appears in speech.

Shall in dialogue is quite infrequent. It appears with no verb phrase modifiers other than one instance of negation, but no phase or aspect.

From this sample, it can be concluded that predictive *shall* is well on the way to becoming obsolete. It has lost its status as an independent part of the modal system and is now best referred to as a stylistic variant of *will* conditioned by the person of its subject or by a desired connotation of prestige socio-educational level or by both. That is, instead of adding to the content of the discourse in which it appears beyond the meaning of *will*, it serves as a means of establishing a certain kind of relationship between the speaker or writer and his listener or reader. I could speak perfectly idiomatic English without ever using another *shall*. This is not the case for *may*, for instance.

There are no instances in my sample of its most common use in speech, interrogations like "shall I close the door?" If there were, they would represent the independent meaning of *shall*, the speaker [or his designate (p. 13)] is the most important guaranteeing factor for the occurrence of the predication. Otherwise stated, assurance of occurrence is marked for speaker's view of the state of the environment.

[1] These are the usual meanings in Shakespeare.

SHOULD

The behavior of *should* is quite unlike that of the modal auxiliaries previously discussed. As we have seen, *shall*, which was originally the form of which *should* was the past, has lost its independent meaning and become a stylistic variant of *will*. A result of this is the fact that meanings which can be interpreted as past forms of *shall* are infrequent. In (223) it is clear that *should* behaves as a stylistic variant of *would* with "I", carrying indications that the speaker has attained a certain educational level.

(223) I *should* be obliged if you could make other arrangements for your daughters. 0220E1K23

Altogether there are six instances of this type, of which all are hypothetical. Only one appears with a subject other than a first-person pronoun (224). This is from a quoted letter and represents a dated form of speech. If it were to occur in a contemporary utterance, it would probably represent the same sort of speaker's guarantee that *shall* was said to show when occurring with a second- or third-person subject. This sentence illustrates the previous statement that the subject's function as guarantor is in large part lost, and the burden falls on the speaker or writer.

(224) . . . that *should* a minister in Boston trust himself to his heart, *should* he "speak without book," and consequently break some law of speech, or be hurried into some daring hyperbole, he *should* find little mercy. 1170E1D05

It is probable that *should* behaves similarly in sentences like (225), where it appears in a result clause. There are six such cases, and all but three are quotations from older sources. Instances of this type of usage may well include stylistic carryovers from Biblical usage giving a feeling of education through their connotations of archaism. The basic notion of guaranteed occurrence is retained, however, so that even these limited instances can be considered past-tense forms of a now-dead predictive *shall*.

(225) . . . is the temperature which must be assumed for the black body in order that the intensity of its radiation *should* equal that of the observed radiation. 1110E1J01

Also derived from the no longer used predictive *shall* are the somewhat more frequent instances of a *should* which acts as nothing but a carrier of non-actuality. It appears most often with "if" (226) or inverted with the subject to carry the meaning of "if". At one time this type of *should* probably functioned in much the same way as heavily hypothetical *would* does now, but with the death of independent *shall*, hypothetical *should* has ceased to carry predictive meaning. The inverted occurrences show this especially clearly, since the hypothesis is expressed only by *should* and the word order, not by other expressed elements. This type of *should* is the only modal which inverts with the subject in anything but interrogation, which is another indication that it is not like the other modals, all of which have their own meanings in addition to the meaning of the non-actual past.

(226) She did not pause to consider what she would do if her plan *should* fail; 0750E1N08

There are four examples of hypothetical *should* which follows "that" and a verb expressing desire (227), and two follow close equivalents. These all seem considerably closer to the predictive meaning of the now-defunct *shall* than those discussed previously, but because the hypothetical element remains very strong, it is convenient to classify these with the hypothetical *should* which follows "if".

(227) . . . but because He pitied him, (and did not desire)[2] that he *should* continue a sinner for ever, nor that the sin which surrounded him *should* be immortal, . . . 1140E1D04

The overwhelming majority of the occurrences of *should* do not represent the past of predictive *shall* in any way. They are so widely separated in meaning that it is necessary for the first time to speak of a modal auxiliary which does not have a single meaning, be it unitary (*can*, *will*) or variable (*may*). Most of the occurrences of *should* carry a *normative* basic meaning, which can be stated as follows: the predication conforms to the writer's or speaker's view of some aspect(s) of the environment.

Most of the minor variations in meaning take place in the portion of the definition which refers to "aspect(s) of the state of the world", with the result that this definition may seem rather open and loose. However, it is only this definition which constitutes the lowest common denominator of all the occurrences of normative *should.* The particular portion of the state of the world which the speaker or writer actually views in any given sentence is determined by other elements of context. Therefore, in a sense any of the different aspects which complete the definition of normative *should* may be seen as something like overtones, except for the fact that they are not independent variations of the entire meaning but rather a seemingly infinitely variable set of complements.

There is another point of some looseness in the definition. The speaker's or writer's view includes attitudes and emotions as well as what he might consider a more "objective" structuring of the reality that presents itself to him. This means, for instance, that when the aspect of the state of the world in question consists of a moral code, it may be the moral code of the speaker's culture or it may be more the speaker's own addition to that moral code. Sentences (228) and (229) exemplify morality in the "aspect of the state of the world" position.

(228) But in any event, full credit *should* be given to the Cost Section for its express and overt recognition of a vital distinction too often ignored. . . 0500E1J50

(229) . . . and I believe there is little difference of opinion that wherever possible a

[2] Words enclosed in parentheses appeared in all capital letters.

local school board *should* devise and effect a plan of desegregation. 0960E1J48

This type is very infrequent in unambiguous form; there are some other sentences which are ambiguous and could be interpreted either as referring to morality or as referring to some other aspect. Such a case is (230), which is typical of such ambiguous instances. Here the modal may be interpreted either as referring to a public morality or to the writer's view of the way to accomplish his aim most effectively.

(230) Even though in civil rights legislation in 1957 and 1960 the provision for the Attorney General to act was eliminated, *should* we nevertheless support such a clause? 1540E1J48

Occasionally *should* expresses the writer's view about someone's best advantage, usually that of the addressee (231). Other types of relevant aspect include the speaker's view of the importance of his work (232), his knowledge of how to accomplish an end (233), his knowledge of certain facts not accessible to the addressee (234), his opinion about the best ordering of a certain set of facts or activities (235), etc.

(231) . . . if you haven't made avocado a part of your diet yet, you really *should.* 1160E1E02

(232) . . . sedulously fostered by all too many academics who mistakenly believe that their frivolous efforts *should* be taken seriously because they are expressed with that dreary solemnity. . . 0150E1J57

(233) For treatment of shipping fever, this level *should* be fed at the onset of the disease symptoms until symptoms disappear. 0400E1E27

(234) . . . the secretary's tone indicated that an appointment at such short notice was a concession for which Madden *should* be duly grateful. 0560E1L15

(235) . . . if one is permitted to speculate, potential pathology *should* be included in this statement as well. 0720E1J12

In items (232) and (234) above it may have been noticed that the writer of the text is not the one whose view is represented by *should.* In the first case it is the academician who considers his own work important, and in the second it is the secretary who has special knowledge. Indirect discourse and interrogation seem to constitute the only circumstances under which *should* refers to the viewpoint of anybody but the actual writer or speaker of the verb phrase. The writer may have the agreement of society at large, as in (236), but nonetheless, the one whose viewpoint is usually expressed is the writer.

(236) And after a while, he dried his tears and walked the deck as a captain *should* with assurance and dignity. 1240E1P07

Indirect discourse is reported speech, so the *should* used in it simply represents the viewpoint of the speaker or writer who is being quoted. It is therefore better, perhaps, but far more cumbersome, to refer to the one whose viewpoint is expressed by *should* as "a speaker" or "the speaker or someone explicitly or implicitly designated by the speaker" (this will be the understanding when the term "the speaker" is used from here on to refer to part of the definition of a modal auxiliary).

There is sometimes ambiguity as to whether *should* is the past of *shall* or whether it is normative. In (237) if *should* is normative then it refers to the writer's opinion about the proper way to understand general phonologic theory. Otherwise it is a stylistic variant of *would*.

(237) We *should* expect that general phonologic theory should be as adequate for tone as for consonants and vowels, . . . 0370E1J34

The only overtone of *should*, one of high probability, may be defined as follows: the occurrence of the predication will result in the predication's being identical to the speaker's or writer's view as to the probable result of a certain set of causal factors. Although fairly substantial alterations have been made in the expression of the basic meaning, the notion of high probability certainly remains a derived meaning. Furthermore, no specific conditioners can be found in the context, though it is certainly something about the context that determines the use of the overtone. The presence of *will* in the definition accounts for the fact that this is the only type of *should* which shows time function as it appeared with *will*. Thus (238) has future time function, and (239) is time-neutral.

(238) Shayne looked at his watch. That wasn't too far from Fifth Street, and *should* allow him to make Scotty's Bar by midnight. 0080E1L05

(239) Since the absorption of radio waves in rocklike material varies with wave length, it *should* be possible to sample the temperature variation at different depths. . . 0660E1J01

In (240) the verb phrase may be considered an ellipsis of "(There is no reason why) you should complain" or it may be paraphrased as follows: Your complaining (a most hypothetical action under the circumstances) does not conform to my view of the circumstances. The negation is not expressed; it is carried by the irony (which would be expressed through context and intonation). This type of *should* is used only in conversation (here it appeared in dialogue).

(240) "How often do they add up to headlines? You *should* complain." 0930E1L05

Although we know that *should* was originally the past tense of *shall*, expressing temporal remoteness as well as non-actuality, the situation has changed considerably. Now even in the cases where *should* acts as the past tense of *shall* it has no reference to past time. It is a stylistic variant of non-actual *would* rather than past-time *would*. The normative instances come still closer to the establishment of *should* as an independent modal auxiliary, for they have no relation to the tense of the preceding discourse and may appear without reference to the rules of sequence of tense. As a result, it is possible to have sentences where the environment is a present-tense one and those in which the environment is past. Because normative *should*, then, is no longer a past tense form, it is not surprising to note that it has lost nearly all of its non-actuality and is now a statement of the speaker's or writer's opinion or structuring of the aspect(s) of the state of the world concerned in the given sentence.

Despite the fact that *should* as the past of *shall* is not used, at least in this corpus, with past time meaning, its behavior with phase remains unchanged in the one instance where past tense *should* and phase appear in the same verb phrase (241). In (241a) the old ambiguity of past tense forms of modals reappears; it is possible to interpret past tense as conditioned by sequence of tense or as expressive of hypothetical non-actuality. As before, the ambiguity is relieved by the use of "have", which leaves no room for doubt that the predication is to be placed in a time prior at least to that of the utterance.

(241) During these first days of the trial I didn't have as much time to commiserate with Viola as I *should* have liked. 1420E1R01

(241a) . . . I didn't have as much time to commiserate with Viola as I *should* like (to have).

For normative *should*, "have" provided whatever past tense effect is necessary. Since normative *should* has become a one-form modal, it needs the other verb phrase element to give it a temporal reference that its normally completely neutral nature would not provide. It is here that the fading element of non-actuality is most clearly preserved, for all of the phase-marked instances of *should* carry the special hypothetical notion of contrary to fact.

(242) This suggests that the sampling period, particularly at the more distant locations, *should* have been increased. 1000E1J08

The behavior of *should* in direct and indirect questions with interrogative pronouns and adverbs is of considerable interest. The most frequently occurring of the question-words is "why" (243), which may be paraphrased as "my wanting the pictures conforms to your view of what portion of the state of the world?". Thus this kind of interrogation means that the meaning of the modal auxiliary is affected because attention is drawn to its incompleteness. Sentence (244) on the other hand, contrasts with those having "why" in that the only constants are the writer's view and the most effective way of achieving the goal, the second being the aspect of the state of the world of which the writer holds an opinion. "Who", "what", and "where" ask about that which must do the conforming to the writer's view. "How" also refers to the predication which must conform to the writer's view; essentially (245) asks "what arrangement of sharing most closely conforms to my idea of an equitable distribution of the increase?" In the case of "why" the speaker or writer does not refer to his own views of the aspect(s) of the state of the world in general. On the other hand, "who", "what", and "how" all presume agreement by the addressee with the speaker or writer as far as the view is concerned; attention is focussed on the other matters.

(243) Why *should* I want pictures of an empty room now? 0160E1P03
(244) It changes the answers to "Who *should* do what, and where?". 0380E1E35
(245) . . . the problem of agreeing how an increase in profit margins related to a productivity increase *should* be shared. 1470E1J41

There are only six instances of contracted *shouldn't*, of which one is a stylistic variant of *wouldn't* (246), and the rest express various types of normative *should*, with one representative of the overtone of high probability. For normative *should* it makes no difference which element of the verb phrase the "not" belongs with. On the other hand, item (246) shows that when the past tense of predictive *shall* is negated, the "not" goes with the remainder of the predication and not with *should*. This is as it should be, for we saw that negated predictive *will* behaved similarly.

(246) "I *shouldn't* like to have to write you up for insubordination as well as dereliction of duty." 1170E1L17

We have seen, then, that the meaning of *should* is not as simple as that of the other modals and certainly not as tidy. It is necessary to speak of two major meaning groups, one of which is the normative meaning with its one overtone and many contextual variants, and the other is the group of meanings which derive from the past of predictive *shall*. One of these is the stylistic variant of *would* which corresponds to the only use for *shall* appearing in this corpus. The other is the *should* of pure hypothesis, where the modal remains as a carrier of the effects of the non-actual past and loses most if not all of its independent meaning. Finally, there are a few residual cases of a predictive non-actual *should* appearing in certain limited environments.

6. OUGHT

As far as can be determined, *ought to* is a synonym for normative *should* in almost every respect. The exceptions to total mutual interchangeability are few and usually explainable without difficulty. An attempt to substitute *ought to* for every occurrence of *should* proved that non-normative *should* is never interchangeable with *ought to*, and that *ought to* may be put in the place of *should* in ambiguous sentences, but only to the extent that part of the ambiguity involves normative *should* (247), (247a). This further supports a rather sharp division between normative *should* and the other types.

(247) "I don't understand why a white hotel *should* be down here." 1410E1K04
(247a) I don't understand why a white hotel *ought to* be down here.

The only other case where *ought to* cannot be substituted for *should* is the single ironic instance (240). Here the meanings of the two modal auxiliaries remain essentially the same, but the combination of *ought to* and the environmental factors like intonation (which is not shown in the written representation) and context does not happen to result in the same effect as the combination of these factors and *should*. This may be a result of the fact that *should* is, after all, still a recognizable past form of *shall*, and the normative version is a relatively recent member of the group of verbs which have no marked past, so that it probably retains more of the notion of hypothesis even in its now temporally neutral normative meaning. It may be just this small element of surviving non-actuality (which we also saw in the fact that normative *should* is always contrary to fact with "have") which accounts for the fact that *should* can be ironic and *ought to* cannot. The situation in (248) is related in that replacing the *should* with *ought to* makes the sentence entirely normative, while in its original form it had enough of the hypothetical sense of *should* to make it clear that the two modals do not always mean the same thing; that is, they may be contrastive even when *should* is strongly normative.

(248) The clerk impressed this upon me: that I *should* not arrive in the hall before ten o'clock. 1230E1N06

In some cases substitution was either very awkward or rather uncomfortable. The very awkward cases include required inversion, that is, questions of most sorts and one instance of indirect negation (249). The discomfort involved in inverting *ought* and the subject probably explains the total absence of any sort of inversion among the sentences containing *ought to*. Even in the questions in this group of sentences inversion is avoided (250), (251). The use of *ought to* in ordinary questions would be an indicator of very careful style, and the tendency to relieve the awkwardness by saying "didn't he ought to . . . ?" reveals a pressure to class *ought to* with the catenatives, all of which also retain the particle "to". *Ought to* is nevertheless still best considered a modal auxiliary on grounds of both morphology (no person or number inflection, highly defective) and syntax (may occupy the modal slot in a verb phrase and does not combine with other modals, forms what past it has with "have").

(249) Nor, when we recollect how sensitive were the emotions of the old Puritan stock in regard to the recent tides of immigration, *should* we be astonished that their thin lips were compressed... 1450E1D05

(250) What *ought to* be, what is his potential role as a force for constructive social change? 0190E1D12

(251) No longer did the sovereign look to the law of nations to determine what he *ought to* do; 0760E1J42

Ought to is mildly uncomfortable with anything that necessitates interpolation of some element other than the sentence subject between *ought* and *to*. In (252) the element is "not". It is significant that there are no instances of direct negation among the sentences containing *ought to*, but one of the two indirectly negated occurrences has "never" between the verbal and the particle (253). Other adverbial elements have this effect also (254).

(252) They *should* not be sad. 0780E1M01

(253) . . . underneath it I could see his tie, knotted, ready to be slipped over his head, a black badge of frayed respectability that *ought* never *to* have left his neck. 0280E1N06

(254) You *should* also begin this exercise with a very light barbell... 1800E1E01

The meaning of *ought to* seems to be identical with that of normative *should* (255), (256). The overtone of probability occurs twice, once with future time function (257) and once with neutral time function (258). *Ought to* expresses no temporal relations at all, so it is put into preceding time by phase, which occurs only in sentence (253). A passive verb phrase appears twice, and there is one case each of aspect and pre-predicate use.

(255) . . . no man, however criminal, *ought to* suffer the penalty without a fairer trial. 0360E1J58

(256) ". . . He's got to thaw slow. You *ought to* know that." 1440E1K24

(257) "I read it, yes. This *ought to* simplify Tolley's life." 0040E1P03

(258) It will be seen that where the scope is similar, the Athabascan ratios come out

somewhat higher (as indeed they *ought to* with a total ratio of 2.8 as against 3.5 or 4:5)... 0400E1J35

There are only 23 occurrences of *ought to.* There were no factors to be found which could indicate that there is a stylistic or other conditioner determining the use of one or the other (the proportions of dialogue uses were roughly equivalent, the types of sources seemed to be in about the same proportions, and both modals preceded the same verbs (259), (260). All this might seem to support the moribundity of *ought to.* However, there seems to be no evidence for such a conclusion in my speech or that of my associates. As far as I can tell, normative *should* and *ought to* are in free variation except in certain kinds of construction made awkward by the "to", instances where hypothesis is important to the meaning of *should,* and perhaps some cases where sentence rhythm is significant.

(259 "Of course, there was nothing you could do, but you still *ought to* be ashamed of yourself for letting it happen"... 0190E1P17

(260) You get a good, loyal husband – smack! – and you fall for a pass by his own nephew! You *should* – smack! – be ashamed of yourself. 1570E1N18

7. MUST

The meaning of *must* is unitary, relatively simple and clearly evident in all the sentences where the modal appears. It comes out to be something like "the predication is required by some aspect(s) of the state of the world". The aspect(s) of the state of the world can include rule or regulation (261), the nature of a sound piece of work (262), or a change in the attitude of those among whom the speaker lives (263). Other meanings include the best or only way to achieve an end (264) and the obviousness of the conclusion presented by the data (265).

(261) The officer had told him that both lists *must* be checked. 0370E1K21

(262) For more explicit expositions, one *must* distinguish different types of analyses. 0180E1J50

(263) "And also, sir, two articles which were considered souvenirs now *must* be regarded in another light entirely. An African knife and battle-ax are at this moment being sharpened..." 0260E1P07

(264) To be perfectly free, the young man *must* revel in the great kingdom of thought and imagination; ... 0330E1E26

(165) In considering BW defense, it *must* be recognized that a number of critical meteorological parameters *must* be met for an aerosol to exhibit optimum effect. 0440E1J08

A frequent relevant aspect is one which comes very close to the meaning of the sequential overtone of *will*. It indicates that the predication is a logical conclusion required by the premises, and it looks like the prediction in implications when *will* is used to express the conclusion. The difference between the two is really no more and no less than the difference between assurance of occurrence and requirement of occurrence. This type of *must* appears almost always in technical uses, especially in mathematical texts, and it is always accompanied by some word or phrase like "therefore", "hence" (266), or "thus" that expresses the logical relation between the premises and the conclusion containing *must*. These words do not condition this meaning alone. Other aspects may well overrule the one of logical requirement even when these words are present (267).

(266) Hence Γ *must* have either a regulus of **F-fold secants or a regulus of **F-fold secants. 1380E1J21

(267) "It is getting dark, so you *must* take your flashlight when you go."

There are three uses. They have been classed as uses rather than overtones because, while the only explicit conditioners in the written context are the lexical verbs for the first two uses and perhaps pronoun subjects, each is closely associated with a single, limited, and highly specific situation. All three involve close specifications of the aspect(s) of the definition. The first is concession, in which the aspect of the environment requiring the predication is honesty [in (268) it is intellectual honesty]. Sentence (268) is one of the three cases where this use appears with an impersonal passive; otherwise the subject is in the first person (269). Other lexical verbs with which this use appears are "say", "concede", "admit", and "express". *Must* under such circumstances may carry the feeling of reluctance (perhaps politely simulated reluctance) to comply with the requirement.

(268) While it *must* be said that these same Protestants have built some new churches during this period,... 0850E1D03
(269) I *must* plead guilty to a special sympathy for nomias. 1590E1J10

There are two instances of a deferent use in which the addressee is required either to forgive (270) or to understand (271) the speaker. Both instances have a second-person subject and are probably of the same level of politeness as the *will* of "won't you come in". Also similar in a sense to *will*, but this time more in meaning, are the two instances in which the addressee's insistence requires the predication. Again both are second-person sentences. One of the auxiliaries is in an "if"-clause (272), and the other is in a question (273).

(270) You *must* forgive me if I seem to dwell too much on her physical aspects but I am an artist, ... 0430E1N18
(271) "You *must* understand, I haven't been in this state too long..." 1490E1L23
(272) "If you *must* know, I don't get along with the landlord..." 0550E1L23
(273) "Captain ... Jan ... *must* you go inside Majdanek? The stories ... Everyone really knows what is happening there." 1240E1K17

We have already seen that *must* is similar to normative *should* in the fact that it refers to relevant aspects of the environment. It is similar also in the fact that it, too, has a single overtone, one of high probability. It reads something like the following: "the predication is required by my view of the probable consequences of all the relevant factors." The reason this *must* is still modal is the fact that it is the speaker's view that provides the weak point in the certainty of the predication. It is, of course, just this weak point which differentiates the meaning of the overtone from the basic meaning; on the other hand, it is the basic meaning from which the overtone is derived that differentiates probable *must* from probable *should* and makes it expressive of higher probability. Of course, as always, any other type of *must* carries with it the idea of speaker's view – this is one of the most important characteristics of the modal auxiliaries – but in most cases it is not specifically relevant to the definition of the verbal as it is in the cases of normative *should*, *ought to*, and probable *must* and thus is not semantically marked.

There are 34 occurrences of phase-marked *must*, and in all cases the modal expresses high probability (274). It is interesting to note that phase has no effect at all on the temporal function of the modal. The notion of high probability remains entirely neutral as far as time is concerned, and what follows is put into a time prior to that of the discourse or the utterance. This is also the case in the two instances in which there is also aspect-marking (275), (276). In (277) we can see phase performing the same functions in past context; current relevance is also an obvious portion of its meaning here.

(274) The cars *must* have had their gas pedals pushed down to the floor boards. 1330E1L04
(275) Her hair was dyed, and her bloom was fading, and she *must* have been crowding forty, . . . 0880E1K22
(276) Mark's thoughts *must* have been keeping silent pace beside his own, climbing the same crags in dirty white sneakers, . . . 1460E1K23
(277) He made the mistake of answering in an offhand way, and instantly realized that his skepticism *must* have showed in his face or voice. 1330E1L23

Must and normative *should* are similar in that both have but one form and are therefore indifferent to the past-tense distinctions which the dual-form modals express. In (278) *must* appears in a past context, one which would require a sequence-of-tense past form for *can*, *may*, *will*, or *shall*. In (279) the past would have to be hypothetical, but here it is not. In (280) any specifically future reference is certainly a result of the presence of "eventually". On the other hand, in (281) and (282) the juxtaposition of *must* and normative *should* serves to make the difference between their meanings clear. *Must* expresses requirement; *should* indicates that the speaker or writer holds the action desirable for some reason but does not require it.

(278) The expedient thing – yes, very true, one *must* make do as one could, in some situations. 0950E1L08
(279) If she, Pamela, were being held responsible for his crimes, then hers *must* be the final act of expiation. 0350E1N08
(280) Tests recorded certain essential facts about Helva that Central *must* eventually learn. 0220E1M05
(281) . . . so is the carefree attitude toward what a boatman may and may not do; *must* and *should* do. 1100E1E06
(282) *Must* or *should* the Federal government help? 1930E1J48

In all cases negation applies to the rest of the predicate and not to the modal (for negation of *must* one has to use the educated *need not*, which is equivalent to "don't need to" – it is, by the way, interesting to note that while *must* is negated by *need not*, *need* can not be negated by *must not*). *Must not* is also used to negate permissive *may*.

(283) No, she would not pretend modesty, but neither *must* she be crudely bold. 0590E1K20

(284) "I *mustn't* tell, I *mustn't* tell", she repeated to herself. 1300E1K20

(285) But we *must* not forget man's soul. 1410E1D06

8. DARE, NEED

There are nineteen examples altogether of *dare*, of which only two are clearly modal (both are from the same religious source) (286), (287). Both are negated by "not". There are three sentences where the verb seems to act as a special kind of catenative taking an unmarked infinitive, for the modal slot is already occupied, and "would dare + infinitive" does not seem to be the same sort of usage as the dialectical "might could". Of these, two follow a negated *would* and two follow *do*, as in sentence (288).

(286) ... he *dare* not be a cosmic aeon that swoops to earth for a while ... 0080E1D04

(287) These two aspects of death cannot be successfully separated, but they *dare* not be confused or identified. 1390E1D04

(288) We are left helpless to cope with it because we do not *dare* speak of it as anything real ... 1040E1D01

In one of two ambiguous sentences one (289) *dare* acts as a propredicate (something it could do either as a modal or as a catenative), and in the other (290) the writer's awkward but ingenious style leaves a question as to whether he intended a following "to". In view of the placement of the negator, this *dare* is probably best considered modal, though such an interpretation results in a disturbance of parallelism. In the first of these two sentences, "don't you dare" has almost assumed the status of a fixed phrase for the imperative.

(289) "I could walk out the door." "Don't you *dare*." 0580E1P22

(290) ... how clearly he saw the cultural defection of experimentation as an escape for those who *dare* not or prefer not to face the discipline of modern traditionalism. 0820E1E22

Dare generally requires a personal or personalized subject just by virtue of its emotional significance, but in the one source that has used modal *dare* we find that it is "aspects of death" which "dare not be confused ..." (287). The writer probably meant "but we *dare* not confuse or identify ..." This is possibly further evidence of the breakdown in the use of this verb; for one thing, if it were somewhat more frequent, such an error would probably not have been made.

We need pay no further attention to modal *dare* in view of its extreme infrequency.

NEED

The overwhelming evidence here points to the conclusion that *need* has become a catenative lexical verb. Of the 23 intransitive verbal uses, only four are modal (291) and all of them are negative. They occur either with "not" (two cases) or with an indirect negator like "no" or "only". Otherwise there are two cases of a mock-broken English use in which *need* is negated by "don't" or "no" (292), but the following infinitive is unmarked. It is possible that the author of the selection intended a foreign-sounding verb negator in "no" due to the influence of imitations of Spanish English. It is interesting that this portion of the language should have been chosen to represent the breakdown of an otherwise suspiciously sophisticated English; perhaps the author felt that a person not too sure of his English would be more likely than not to have trouble with such a transitional and unstable feature of the verb system.

(291) Note that we *need* not know the value of *P*, for the experiment to be binomial. 0990E1J19

(292) You don't *need* worry, Angelo. 0680E1L08

(293) No *need* leave a note with it, either – 1310E1L08

This is especially likely in view of the fact that seven of the eleven occurrences of *need to* are negative, so that negative "don't need to" and "need not" seem equally usable. The difference is probably stylistic, since three of the four modal uses appear in technical text, while most of the catenatives are in narrative or dialogue.

9. CONCLUSION

We can conclude, then, with a brief summary of some of the findings of this study. *Dare* and *need* are used so strikingly infrequently that for the purposes of this analysis they are said to be no longer in use as modal auxiliaries. Rather, they are nearly full members of the set of catenative verbs, many of which have meanings very close to or at least somewhat related to those of the modal auxiliaries. *Need not* (or *need* with indirect negation) may be considered one way of negating *must*, since, as we have seen, *must* itself is not negated when with *not*. In this case, *need* may be described as having only one foot in the grave and so probably should be given a meaning to differentiate it from *must*. Twaddell's method of differentiation is probably as good as any; *need* brings in the speaker's or writer's opinion, which *must* does only in its overtone of probability. *Need* does not express probability of any kind, so there is no danger of ambiguity resulting from overlap of meanings. A frequent aspect of the state of the world affecting the requirement expressed in *need* is the subject's best advantage.

The other modals, *can*, *may*, *will*, *shall*, *should*, *ought to*, and *must*, all have a basic meaning which is unitary for all but *may*, and the first four have the past-tense forms *could*, *might*, *would*, and *should*, which add the remote meaning of the past to the original meaning of the present-tense form. The meaning of *may* is a two-dimensional continuum on which any occurrence can be located approximately. The dimensions involved are the occurrential and the circumstantial; the latter is equivalent to the meaning of *can*, and the former is closely related to the meaning of *will*. The basic meaning of *will* is predictive, referring to guaranteed occurrence; and running through all its variations is the contextually determined time-function which determines whether or not the predication has any temporal relation to what surrounds it or to the utterance. Time function applies to the occurrential portion of *may* as well. *Shall* is primarily a stylistic variant of *will*, and normative *should* and *ought to* are synonymous.

Table 2 shows relationships of the modal auxiliaries. *Can*, *may*, and *will* are connected through *may* by their expressing the same dimensions of meaning. In addition, there is one overtone of *can* which has a strongly occurrential sense and is therefore connected closely to the occurrential end of the continuum which is the meaning of *may*. There is a strong connection between *will* and *shall*, which in the

TABLE 1

The Meanings of the Modals

CAN	nothing in the state of the world prevents the predication: A. there are certain positive qualities of the subject such that the way is cleared for the predication; B. no lack of permission prevents the predication; C. nothing in the state of the world prevents the occurrence of the predication.
MAY	nothing in the state of the world prevents the predication, and furthermore there is no guarantee that the predication will not occur.
WILL	the occurrence of the predication is guaranteed, either in a concrete (future time function) or a general (neutral time function) context: A. subject's volition has something to do with the guarantee; B. the predication is a natural consequence or concomitant of another factor or predication.
SHALL	same as *will*, except used with first person subject and carries stylistic notion of education involving exposure to prescriptive grammar (this is the only current usage of *shall* in the corpus; in speech it is also used with second- and third-person subjects to indicate that the speaker or someone designated by the speaker guarantees the predication.)
SHOULD - OUGHT TO	the predication conforms to the speaker's or writer's view of some aspect(s) of the state of the world: A. the occurrence of the predication will conform to the speaker's or writer's view of the probable result of the relevant factors.
MUST	the predication is required by some aspect(s) of the state of the world: A. the occurrence of the predication is required by the speaker's or writer's view of the probable result of the relevant factors.
(NEED)	the predication is required by the speaker's or writer's view of some aspect(s) of the state of the world.

corpus of material under discussion are differentiated only by stylistic considerations, and which in any case are both predictive in nature. The connection, on the other hand, is weaker between *ought-should* and *shall*. The connection here is primarily through the fact that normative *should* and the past-tense form of *shall* are formally alike, and it is not always perfectly clear which is meant (sometimes both may be meant). Both also refer to and are marked for the speaker's view which *is* the aspect of the world assuring the occurrence of the predication, whereas for *should-ought* the two are separate. The normative modals are connected with *must* because they share an overtone of high probability, which in both cases involves the speaker's or writer's view of the relevant aspects of the state of the world. The older grammarians consulted would say that both also indicate the notion of "constraint".

Must and *can* are connected by the fact that both are circumstantial. The difference between them, needless to say, is the fact that for the one the circumstances have the positive effect of requiring the predication, whereas for the other they have the negative effect of leaving the possibility open for its occurrence. It must, however, be added that neither says anything at all about whether the predication occurs; this is the job of *will*.

Joos' modal cube[1] begins to break down as soon as *dare* and *need* are removed from

[1] See Joos (1964), p. 149.

TABLE 2

The Relations between the Modals

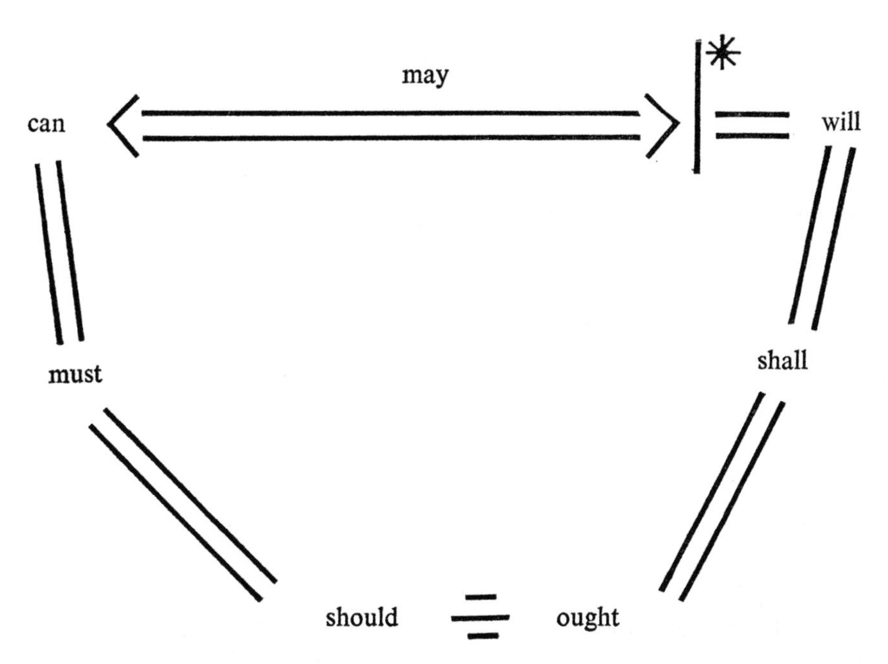

* The meaning of *may* stops short of that of *will* by the breadth of a double negative.

the list of modals. The behavior of *shall*, the equivalence of *should* and *ought to*, and the sliding meaning of *may*, to say nothing of the inapplicability of portions of Joos' meanings of the individual modals, complete the process of the destruction of the cube's applicability to the American Engish of our sample. The arrangement given in Table 2 seems to be the best that can be done as far as geometric representation goes: the modals appear as a circular chain somewhat arranged, which consists of links of varying strengths.

In Table 3 auxiliaries are placed with respect to two major dimensions of meaning, ignoring the past-tense forms. On the horizontal axis the dimension is *contingency*; on the vertical axis it may be called *conditioner*. The relation of each column on the contingency dimension to its neighbor on the right is one of implication. Thus "required predication" implies "non-occurrence not guaranteed" (as well as the following "circumstantially permitted" and "consistent with the conditioner"). Of course, this relation is not reversible; e.g. "consistency" does not imply "circumstantially permitted", etc.

On the vertical axis, the relations are those of marked to unmarked. Beginning with the lowest, we may say that each row represents a marked[2] version of the row

[2] "Marked" refers to restrictions not explicitly indicated in the unmarked forms.

TABLE 3

The Modal System

Conditioner	Contingency			
	required predication	non-occurrence not guaranteed	predication not prevented	predication conforms
environment	*will* (stylistic *shall*)	*may_1*	*can* *may_2*	5
aspect of environment	*must* (*need not*)	1	3	6
speaker's view of environment	*shall* (*need*)*	2	4 (*dare*)*	*should-ought to*

* Marginal item.

just above it. This means that "speaker's view of an aspect of the nevironment" (abbreviated "speaker's view") may be considered doubly marked or else we may think of "some relevant aspect of the environment" (abbreviated "aspect") as both the marked form of "environment" and the unmarked form for "speaker's view". The distinction is not an important one.

The farther to the right the auxiliary is located, the more modal it is. Thus, *should-ought* is the most modal, since it is farthest to the right and lowest. *Will* is the least modal. The numbering of *may* refers to the two dimensions of the meaning (*may_1* is circumstantial; *may_2* is occurrential), and the meaning used for *shall* is the independent one which does not appear in the corpus but which appears in spoken use.

Each of the numbered spaces in the diagram may be accounted for by at least one row or column by which it is implied or of which it would be a marked form if filled. Thus spaces 1, 2, 3, 4 are implied by the filled spaces of the first column (*must*, *shall*); 3 and 4 would represent marked forms of circumstantial allowance, and 1 and 2 would represent marked forms of occurrential allowance. 5 and 6 are implied by preceding columns.

The absence of fillers for spaces 5 and 6 may be accounted for by the fact that if a predication is consistent with the state of the world, it is not modal. Similarly for an aspect of the state of the world. That means that if a statement of consistency is to be modal, it must carry the notion of the speaker's view with the contingencies which such a limitation entails. *Should-ought* is the element of the system which is marked for limitation to human view of reality and which can therefore be consistent with the environment without canceling modality altogether. For other modal auxiliaries, those in the first two rows, it is understood but not marked that the meaning of the verb includes the fact that any statement it makes is dependent upon the speaker's or writer's view of the state of the world.

TABLE 4

Negation

Negation Refers to the Modal	Either	Negation Refers to the Rest of the Predicate
Cannot, can't		
May-not (permissive)		May not- (occurrential and non-permissive circumstantial)
Will-not (volitional)		Will not- (predictive)
	Should-not- (normative)	Shall not- (compulsive)
	Ought not to	
(Need-not)		Must not-

Appendix A

THE SEMANTICS OF THE MODAL AUXILIARIES IN SHAKESPEARE'S PLAYS

This study was undertaken on a corpus of 22 samples of approximately 500 lines each from the plays of William Shakespeare, representing all periods. It consists of approximately 75,000 words, or the equivalent of a little more than a quarter of the 275-300,000 word corpus used for the preceding study of the semantics of the modal auxiliaries in present-day English (PDE). Comparison is made throughout this paper with the results of the preceding investigation, and the same presuppositions and methods of working were applied. Special terms and presuppositions are described in the introduction to *The Meanings of the Modals in Present-Day American English.* The spelling of the First Folio[1] is kept, except that allographic long ſ is written s.

Abbreviations of plays cited:

AC	*Antony and Cleopatra*	MM	*Measure for Measure*
AYL	*As You Like It*	MND	*Midsummer's Night's Dream*
CE	*Comedy of Errors*	MA	*Much Ado about Nothing*
Co	*Coriolanus*	R2	*Richard II*
C	*Cymbeline*	R&J	*Romeo and Juliet*
H4,1	*Henry IV*, Part I	TS	*Taming of the Shrew*
H5	*Henry V*	T	*The Tempest*
JC	*Julius Caesar*	TA	*Timon of Athens*
KL	*King Lear*	TC	*Troilus and Cressida*
LLL	*Love's Labour's Lost*	2G	*Two Gentlemen of Verona*
M	*Macbeth*	WT	*Winter's Tale*

CAN

In my paper on the modal auxiliaries in PDE, I established a basic meaning and four apparently unconditioned "overtones", or further semantic markings of the basic meaning, for *can.* The basic meaning is "nothing in surrounding circumstances prevents the predication"; the most common of the overtones was one in which surrounding circumstances consisted specifically of a deficiency in knowledge or ability of the subject of the verb: thus, "no deficiency in the subject prevents the predication". Two related overtones were permission and a semi-imperative de-

[1] Helge Kökeritz and C. T. Prouty, eds., *Shakespeare's Comedies, Histories, & Tragedies*, A Facsimile Edition of the First Folio (New Haven, Yale University Press, 1954).

veloping from the permissive; thus, "there is no absence of permission to prevent the predication". The permissive was much more common than the near-imperative *can*. Occasionally there was also what I called "occurrential" *can*, in which reference was made to the occurrence of the action in addition to the usual reference to the state of the world.

By Shakespeare's time today's basic meaning seems to have been firmly established, since, as Table 5 shows, only about a quarter of the instances of *can* could have had any reference at all to knowing either a fact or how to do a given act.[2] An example of *can* expressing possibility because of "gaps in the subject's ignorance" is [1]. Needless to say, for this older meaning a personal or personalized subject is required, but for many of the other instances of "internal" *can* (referring to absence of deficiency in the subject) there are non-personal subjects [2], [3]. Of course there are also many more personal subjects. Thus the many instances of "internal" *can*, whether or not they refer specifically to knowing, are certainly semantically marked overtones of a basic meaning which may refer to any kind of circumstances affecting any kind of subject. The most significant point to be made here is that all types of "internal" *can* account for approximately half the corpus, whereas in PDE they constituted a signif-iciantly smaller fraction (this and other statements about numbers of occurrences of meanings in the PDE corpus are impressionistic). Thus perhaps there can be seen signs of transition from the old meaning to the firmly established new one, with the basic meaning becoming still more dominant by the present day.

[1] Hee hath Ribbons of all the colours i'th Rainebow; Points, more then all the Lawyers in Bohemia, *can* learnedly handle, though they come to him by th'grosse: [WT IV iv 230]

[2] My eares are stopt, & *cannot* hear good newes, So much of bad already hath possest them. [2G III i 206]

[3] And (which is more then all these boasts *can* be)
I am belou'd of beauteous Hermia. [MND I i 112]

The completeness of the changeover is further attested by the fact that occurrential *can* appears in the Early Modern English (EMnE) corpus twice [4], [5]. The second of these examples must be made positive for the occurrence dimension of meaning to be clear. There are also four cases where interpretation of *can* is doubtful; [6], [7], [8] may all be interpreted either as internal *can* or as occurrential *can*. This ambiguity makes them very much like some instances of balanced-meaning *may*. Certainly no such meaning could have appeared when *can* had its earlier basic meaning.

There is also one very modern-looking sentence which expresses nothing less than

[2] In an investigation of approximately 3,500 lines of Old English poetry now in progress, I have found only one instance of the preterite-present verb *cunnan* (*cann*, *cannst*, *cuðe*) used as an auxiliary. Otherwise it seems to refer to knowledge of facts, and this is the meaning which would be carried over into Middle English, when *cann* became primarily an auxiliary. As an auxiliary it meant "know how to", and as a lexical verb it continued to refer to knowing facts or things.

high probability [9]. In modern use, this sense depends entirely on the presence of negation (here it is indirect); to retain the probability meaning in the positive, *could* must be used: "She could be there already" (note the change of adverbs); or else the sentence becomes occurrential: "She can be there already", and normally a little strange-sounding.

[4] How happy some, ore othersome *can* be? [MND I i 240]
[5] But by bad courses may be vnderstood,
That their euents *can* neuer fall out good. [R2 II i 220]
[6] But there is no such man, for brother, men
Can counsaile, and speake comfort to that griefe,
Which they themselues not feele, but tasting it, [MA V i 23]
[7] Once more Ile marke how Loue *can* varry Wit. [LLL IV iii 97]
[8] Things base and vilde, holding no quantity,
Loue *can* transpose to forme and dignity, [MND I i 247]
[9] *Clo*. How long is't since she went to Milford-Hauen?
Pis. She *can* scarse be there yet. [C III v 178]

The greatest difference between PDE and EMnE *can* is the total absence of permissive *can* from the earlier material. This means that, except for the relatively infrequent occurrential *can*, the meanings of *can* and *may* were actually more distinct in Shakespeare's usage than they are today – that is, if Shakespeare was not so well-trained in the schoolroom prohibitions (assuming they existed in his day) that his works are in this respect not a true representation of spoken usage.

Negation with *can* seems to affect the overtones, so that in most (but not all) cases internal and occurrential *can* have only the basic meaning when negated, either directly or indirectly, as we have already seen in [5]. Negation of internal *can* with meaning change is illustrated by [10] and without meaning change by [11]. Item [12] illustrates the plain basic meaning negated; in all cases the meaning of negated *can* is "something prevents the predication".

[10] No good at all that I *can* do for him,
Vnlesse you call it good to pitie him,
Bereft and gelded of his patrimonie. [R2 II i 244]
[11] Romeo, the loue I beare thee, *can* affoord
No better terme then this: Thou art a Villaine. [R&J III i 62]
[12] And built so sheluing, that one *cannot* climbe it
Without apparant hazard of his life. [2G III i 115]

With *could* all the overtones appear. Sentences [13] and [14] represent the occurrences of "internal" *can* in the positive; [15] represents the basic meaning; and [16] illustrates occurrential *can*. As in PDE, past tense with modals is either remote in time (as in [15]) or remote from immediately perceptible reality, i.e. hypothetical (as in [13]). Hypothesis is only slightly more frequent for *could* in all overtones than past time.

[13] Be friends you English fooles, be friends, wee haue French Quarrels enow, if you *could* tell how to reckon. [H5 IV i 223]

[14] This Cloten was a Foole, an empty purse,
There was no money in't: Not Hercules
Could haue knock'd out his Braines, for he had none. [C IV ii 154]

[15] When *could* they say (till now) that talk'd of Rome,
That her wide Walkes incompast but one man? [JC I ii 167]

[16] Or that perswasion *could* but thus conuince me, . . . [TC III ii 164]

Hypothesis tends to add an element of occurrentiality to other types of *can*, much as does the PDE hypothetical past with *might*. This is especially well illustrated by [17]. In PDE the only verb form inverting with its subject to express "if" is *had* (and sometimes *should* in very formal style); however, there is here an instance of inverted hypothetical *could* to constitute the apodosis of a condition [18], and we shall see other modals behaving similarly. Sentence [19] represents the five instances of marked phase with *could* (there were none with present modals), and in it we can see that phase marking, as in PDE, makes the meaning of the past marking unambiguously hypothetical by putting the action into a time previous to that of the utterance (after which it can be currently relevant). This is the most complex verb phrase with *can*; it is marked for tense, polarity[3] (negative), and phase. The passive sentence [20] illustrates that, as in PDE, passive voice, like negation, changes any internal *can* to a semantically unmarked basic meaning.

[17] Oh, I *could* wish this Tauerne were my drumme. [H4, 1 III iii 215]

[18] *Oh, could their Master come, and goe as lightly,*
Himselfe would lodge where (senceles) they are lying. [2G III i 143]

[19] A Taylor Sir, a Stone-cutter, or a Painter, *could* not haue made him so ill, though they had bin but two yeares oth'trade. [KL II ii 55]

[20] Seldome he smiles, and smiles in such a sort
As if he mock'd himselfe, and scorn'd his spirit
That *could* be mou'd to smile at any thing. [JC I ii 222]

MAY

The meaning of *may* in PDE has been found to be best represented on a two-dimensional continuum whose extremes are represented by the basic meaning of *can* and by an occurrential statement something like "the non-occurrence of the predication is not guaranteed". Both dimensions appear in most instances of *may*; they vary in inverse relation. The most frequent mixture is the so-called "balanced meaning", which seems to have nearly equal parts of both dimensions. A semantically marked form

[3] I have adopted the term *polarity* from M. A. K. Halliday, "Grammatical Categories in Modern Chinese", *Transactions of the Philological Society*, 1956, pp. 177-224.

TABLE 5

Frequencies of Meanings in Shakespeare

Modal / meaning	Frequency
CAN	196
basic meaning	89
know (how to)	47
internal	43
occurrential	2
ambiguous	15
COULD	74
basic meaning, hypothetical	25
basic meaning, past	15
know (how to), hypothetical	8
know (how to), past	1
internal, hypothetical	9
internal, past	7
occurrential, hypothetical	3
ambiguous	6
MAY	117
permissive	9
circumstantial	48
balanced	23
occurrential	34
ambiguous	1
MIGHT	50
permissive, hypothetical	1
permissive, past	1
circumstantial, hypothetical	11
circumstantial, past	2
balanced, hypothetical	14
occurrential, hypothetical	19
ambiguous	2
WILL	592
sequential, future	20
sequential, neutral	3
characterizing, future	
characterizing, neutral	12
basic, future	164
basic, neutral	42
volitional, future	176
volitional, neutral	61
ambiguous: predictive or volitional future	114
WOULD	214
sequential, neutral, hypothetical	5
characterizing, neutral, past	1
basic, future, hypothetical	2
basic, neutral, hypothetical	86
basic, future, past	2
basic, neutral, past	8
volitional, neutral, hypothetical	14
volitional, future, past	5
volitional, neutral, past	4
volitionals in which the meaning of past tense is lost	
neutral	23
future	48
ambiguous: volitional or predictive	
neutral, hypothetical	8
future, past	6
SHALL	287
compulsive	177
predictive	69
predictive, compulsive	15
predictive, future	13
predictive, neutral	5
predictive, sequential	8
SHOULD	168
compulsive, hypothetical	8
compulsive, past	6
pure hypothesis	29
normative, neutral	53
normative, future	1
predictive, hypothetical	62
predictive, past	1
predictive, sequential, hypothetical	4
predictive, compulsive hypothetical	1
probability	1
OUGHT	2
MUST	92
requirement	75
probability	17
DARE	23
DURST	7
NEED	4

The order of categories in the listings is (1) underlying meaning of the modal auxiliary, (2) time function, and (3) the meaning of the past tense marker.

of circumstantial *may* is the permissive, for which there are also counterparts in PDE *can*.

Shakespeare's English shows the same range of meaning; it is in relative frequencies that the greatest differences lie. A look at Table 5 shows that of the three main types of *may*, circumstance-heavy items (including permissives) are clearly the most frequent, while balanced meanings run third in frequency rather than first. As in the case of *can*, with its large number of internal items, almost half of which could refer to knowing, this situation looks as if it reflects a drastic change in meaning much more recent in EMnE times than today. At one time, of course, *may* was nothing but circumstantial. Examples [21], [22], and [23] illustrate, respectively, unambiguous circumstance-heavy *may*, the balanced meaning, and occurrence-heavy *may*.

[21] O be thou my Charon,
And giue me swift transportance to those fields,
Where I *may* wallow in the Lilly beds
Propos'd for the deseruer. [TC III ii 10]

[22] Light Wenches *may* proue plagues to men forsworne,
If so, our Copper buyes no better treasure. [LLL IV iii 386]

[23] Farewell at once, for once, for all, and euer.
Well, we *may* meete againe. [R2 II ii 152]

Permissive *may* is, as in PDE, either personal or impersonal. Personally granted persmision is represented by [24]; permission by law or rule is represented by [25]. Another type of very strong circumstantial *may* is represented by [26], in which the meaning of this modal can be interpreted very nearly as an "internal" *can*. Imperative elements appear in [27].

[24] I am good Friends with my Father, and *may* do any thing. [H4, 1 III iii 190]

[25] But though thou art adjudged to the death,
And passed sentence *may* not be recal'd [CE I i 148]

[26] as neerely as I *may*,
Ile play the penitent to you. [AC II ii 107]

[27] That's all one, you shall play it in a Maske, and you *may* speake as small as you will. [MND I ii 48]

The sliding nature of the scale by which the meaning of *may* is represented is instanced by ambiguous items like the following. [28] could be either balanced or circumstance-heavy, and the modal in [29] ranges between permissive and semantically unmarked circumstantial.

[28] Well Brutus, thou art Noble: yet I see,
Thy Honorable Mettle *may* be wrought
From that it is dispos'd: [JC I ii 331]

[29] *Gent*. That Sir, which I will not report after her.
Doct. You *may* to me, and 'tis most meet you should. [M V i 12]

Both ends of the continuum appear in subordinate clauses headed by *that*. Circumstance-heavy *may* is always the modal used in purpose clauses [30]; the occurrential modal may in addition show in optative expressions like [31]. The addition of hypothesis (usually added by tense marking) is clearly a use, occurring with *that* or with inversion of auxiliary and subject.

[30] Spred thy close Curtaine Loue-performing night,
That run-awayes eyes *may* wincke, and Romeo
Leape to these armes, vntalkt of and vnseene, [RJ III ii 7]

[31] Ile write to my Lord she's dead: Oh Imogen,
Safe *mayst* thou wander, safe returne agen. [C III v 133]

There is one instance of a *may* representing an unexpressed verb phrase with a lexical verb of motion [32]. This is much more common with *will* and *shall*, but also occurs with *must*. There is also one possible instance of phase marking with *may*; in [33] either the *may* is permissive and the *have* lexical, or the *may* is either circumstantial or occurrential, and the *have* is either lexical or a marker of phase. Context does not clear the ambiguity in this sentence.

[32] The Moone shines faire,
You *may* away by Night: [H4, 1 III i 144]

[33] My Father Glendower is not readie yet,
Nor shall wee neede his helpe these foureteene dayes:
Within that space, you *may* haue drawne together
Your Tenants, Friends and neighbouring Gentle-men. [H4, 1 III i 89]

Might has the full range of meaning for *may*, but it also has considerably more basically occurrential instances. In line with today's usage, nearly all the instances of *might* are hypothetical; all but one of those having (possible) past-time meaning are circumstantial or permissive. [34] illustrates both hypothetical circumstantial and hypothetical occurrential; [35] is past-sequence permissive; [36] is past-time circumstantial; and [37] is either past-time or hypothetical occurrential. As in PDE, introduction of the tense marker adds an occurrential element even to the circumstantial items.

Balanced meanings also appear. [38] is balanced and either past-time or hypothetical; [39] is hypothetical balanced. In [40] we have occurrential *may* and hypothetical balanced *might* used as equivalents. The most complex verb phrase so far is [41], which is marked for tense, mode, phase, and voice.

[34] Finde
The Ooze, to shew what Coast thy sluggish care
Might'st easilest harbour in. [C IV ii 205]

[35] Thus did he answer me: yet said heereafter,
I *might* know more. [C IV ii 54]

[36] in that dayes feates,
When he *might* act the Woman in the Scene,
He prou'd best man i'th'field, [Co II ii 108]

[37] who wrought with them:
And all things else, that *might*
. . . Say, Thus did Banquo. [M III i 82]

[38] He being thus Lorded,
Not onely with what my reuenew yeelded,
But what my power *might* els exact. [T I ii 115]

[39] And speake of halfe a dozen dang'rous words,
How they *might* hurt their enemies, if they durst. [MA V i 109]

[40] the cry went out on thee,
And still it *might*, and yet it *may* againe, [TC III iii 184]

[41] Marry sir, by my wife, who, if she had bin a woman Cardinally giuen, *might* haue bin accus'd in fornication, adultery, and all vncleanlinesse there. [MM II i 84]

WILL

In the PDE corpus, *will* had two contextually conditioned time functions, neutral and future, divided approximately equally. The basic meaning "the occurrence of the predication is assured" had two areas of overtone meaning, the sequential (in which the guarantee was logical necessity, or laws of cause-and-effect) and the volitional (in which the subject's willingness, intention, or desire was the guaranteeing factor). Some time-neutral basic meanings were descriptive, characterizing the subject of the verb.

All of these meanings appear in the Shakespeare corpus. [42] is future sequential, [43] is a time-neutral basic meaning expressing characterization, and [44] and [45] are time-neutral and time-future basic meaning respectively. Volition is represented by [46] and [47] for neutral and future willingness; by [48] for time-future intention, and by [49] and [50] for time-future and time-neutral wish or desire.

[42] Take him and cut him out in little starres,
And he *will* make the Face of heauen so fine,
That all the world *will* be in Loue with night, [RJ III ii 25]

[43] A Louers eyes *will* gaze an Eagle blinde. [LLL IV iii 334]

[44] vnnaturall deeds
Do breed vnnaturall troubles: infected mindes
To their deafe pillowes *will* discharge their Secrets: [M V i 67]

[45] yet still it's strange
What Clotens being heere to vs portends,
Or what his death *will* bring vs. [C IV ii 233]

[46] I doe not care: *Ile* giue thrice so much Land
To any well-deseruing friend;
But in the way of Bargaine, mark ye me,

Ile cauill on the ninth part of a hayre. [H4, 1 III i 140]

[47] And yet you *will*
stand to it, you *will* not Pocket vp wrong. [H4, 1 III iii 168]

[48] She bids you,
On the wanton Rushes lay you downe,
And rest your gentle Head vpon her Lappe,
And she *will* sing the Song that pleaseth you, [H4, 1 III i 229]

[49] Why sir I trust I may haue leaue to speake,
And speake I *will*. [TS IV iii 80]

[50] He that sweetest rose *will* finde,
must finde Loues pricke, & Rosalinde. [AYL III ii 102]

As usual, the place where there is greatest difference between PDE and Shakespearian usage is in the statistics. Table 6 shows that of the 592 instances of *will*, only 118 are time-neutral, while 474 are time-future. Most of the reason for this is the nature of the context. There was no drama at all in the PDE sample, but it was noted nevertheless that in dialogue the proportion of time-future *will's* was much higher than in ordinary prose. Here most of the dialogue takes place within the reality of the situation set up in the play, so that most instances of *will* appear in sequences of events unique as far as the world of the play is concerned. This means that time-neutral *will* is used only when a speaker is making a generalization. Much the same situation would probably appear in PDE speech and drama; this disparity is a good reason why people insist on calling *will* the "future tense".

More historically significant is the fact that instances of volitional *will* outnumber instances of PDE basic, sequential, and characterizating *will* 279 to 241. This seems a certain indication of transition between the old purely volitional meaning and the new, predictive significance dominant today. But the Shakespearian situation shows more than transition: the small size of the difference is also significant. It looks very much as if there is no way to describe either area of meaning as basic here, since prediction is numerically secondary; but on the other hand, prediction does not always imply volition (in PDE the overtones always carry some element of the basic meaning).

The absence of a clearcut basic meaning for *will* is reflected by 114 ambiguous items, all time-future and almost all in the first person. These may be interpreted either as basic meanings or as expressions of volition, and there is nothing to cause the analyst to favor one interpretation over another. By far the most common type of volition here is intention [51], but there are also a few instances of willingness, as in, [52]. As in PDE, much of this ambiguity is connected with the unique position of a first person subject as both guarantor and actor of the predication (and volition may actually be seen as a special kind of subject's assurance). [53] shows how closely linked this kind of ambiguity is with a first person subject.

[51] Heark, she speaks, I *will* set downe what comes from her, to satisfie my remem-
brance the more strongly. [M V i 30

[52] I *will* do so: but looke you Cassius,
The angry spot doth glow on Caesars brow, [JC I ii 198]

[53] But I *will* tarry, the Foole *will* stay,
And let the wiseman flie; [KL II v 85]

Because the two meaning areas are related, it is difficult to think of *will* as being split in two like PDE *should.* Instead, perhaps the situation must be described as one of competition between two areas of meaning, neither of which is dominant at present. In [54], the interplay between the volitional (intention) and the predictive futures emphasizes the relationship between the two and provides support for an eventual shift whereby prediction becomes basic.

[54] *Lep.* I am not so well as I should be: But *Ile* ne're out. [AC II vii 36]
Enob. Not till you haue slept: I feare you'*l* bee in till then.

There are four places where an interpretation of inanimate volition is possible. [55] illustrates this. Another instance of volition is a polite use, here represented by the first *will* in [56], which makes use of willingness. This was seen in PDE to appear in interrogative expressions, both positive and negative; this is also the case in Shakespeare's English.

[55] Yon are three, that Rome should dote on:
Yet by the faith of men, we haue
Some old Crab-trees here at home,
That *will* not be grafted to your Rallish. [Co. II i 202]

[56] *Will* you sitte downe with me, and wee two, *will* raile
against our Mistris the world, and all our miserie. [AYL III ii 262]

In one sentence, anomalous as far as PDE usage is concerned, there is what seems to be an ingenious use of time function. In [57] we would expect a volitional *would* with *were* by the rules of unreal past sequence. As noted for PDE, however, the time function would automatically be neutral because of the type of context created by unreal past. What the unmarked form does is, if not cause it to be future, at least allow a future interpretation.

[57] *Ile* hold my minde were she an Ethiope. [MA V iv 40]

Negation with predictive *will* is immediate or eventual with no meaning difference [58]. When *will* is volitional, negation may be either immediate or eventual, with different effects. Sentence [59] provides a convenient ambiguity: if negation is immediate, then *will not* means "not willing to"; if negation is eventual, then *will not* means "wish not to". In some cases negation forces a positive volitional expressing desire to weaken to a volitional expressing (lack of) willingness [60].

[58] A most manly wit Margaret, it *will* not hurt a woman: [MA V ii 16]
[59] You'*ll* not be periur'd, 'tis a hatefull thing:
Tush, none but Minstrels like of Sonnetting. [LLL IV iii 157]
[60] 'Tis a fault I *will* not change, for your best vertue: I am wearie of you. [AYL III ii 267]

There is one instance of *will* in a verb phrase also marked for aspect [61] and several where no lexical verb is expressed at all (these are not propredicates, since the lexical verb does not appear before *will* is used). Most of the omitted verbs are verbs of motion followed by a prepositional phrase or an adverb of motion like *away*, as in [62], but there are a few in which the implied verb is *have* [63].

[61] Doing is actiuitie, and he *will* still be doing. [H5 III vii 100]
[62] Well: I *will* for refuge straight to Bristoll Castle,
The Earle of Wiltshire is alreadie there. [R2 II ii 138]
[63] For you shall hop without my custome sir:
Ile none of it; hence, make your best of it. [TS IV iii 106]

The most striking feature of *would* in PDE is the effect which hypothetical past marking has on time function. Marking for hypothesis makes the immediate context of the verb phrase a general, non-unique one, with the result that, as a rule, hypothetical *would* is time-neutral. This is also clearly the case for Shakespeare's English as well, as Table 6 demonstrates. All meanings and overtones of *will* are represented by hypothetical, time-neutral examples, and prediction, volition, and characterization all appear in past-time instances with both time functions. One of the very rare time-future predictive instances is [64]; a time-future volitional is [65]. [66] is the only instance of a characterizing *would*.

[64] I knew 't*would* be a bald conclusion: but soft, who wafts vs yonder. [CE II ii 110]
[65] There art thou happy. Tybalt *would* kill thee.
But thou slew'st Tybalt, there art thou happie. [RJ III iii 160]
[66] when thou didst not (Sauage)
Know thine owne meaning; but *wouldst* gabble, like
A thing most brutish, I endow'd thy purposes
With words that made them knowne: [T I ii 419]

The most striking thing about the Shakespeare corpus as far as *would* is concerned is the large number (74) of volitional instances which are very archaic in PDE. These behave normally as far as time function is concerned: [67] is time-neutral; [68] is time-future. The remarkable thing about these instances is the fact that the meaning of the past tense should by all rights be hypothetical and probably once was. If this were still the case, however, then future time function, rather than being much more frequent than neutral time function, should be nonexistent. The decay of the hypothetical past meaning in such cases is demonstrated by the presence of both time functions in plenty and several cases of archaic volitional *would* in parallel construction with a present modal or lexical verb, both of which are illustrated in [69]. Thus any meaning for the past marker to be found in such volitionals is residual and often adds little more than a note of deference. "Fain" is often but not always used to mark such volitionals; only in [70] does it clear a real ambiguity.

[67] Our feares in Banquo sticke deepe,
And in his Royaltie of Nature reignes that
Which *would* be fear'd. [M III i 48]

[68] Say to the King, I *would* attend his leysure,
For a few words. [M III ii 3]

[69] I thinke not of them:
Yet when we can entreat an houre to serue,
We *would* spend it in some words vpon that Businesse,
If you *would* graunt the time. [M II i 22]

[70] and as I
told you, hee put it by once: but for all
that, to my thinking, he *would* faine haue had it. [JC I ii 256]

As in the case of *will*, many of the first-person uses of *would* are ambiguous as to interpretation as predictives or volitionals or both. [71] illustrates this with the first person; [72] shows one of the six third-person instances, all of which were in indirect quotations.

[71] And I another,
So wearie with Disasters, tugg'd with Fortune,
That I *would* set my Life on any Chance,
To mend it or be rid on't. [M III i 110]

[72] I heard him sweare,
Were he to stand for Consull, neuer *would* he
Appeare i'th'Market place, nor on him put
The Naples Vesture of Humilitie, [Co II i 257]

Also different from today's usage is *would* in an *if*-clause. Today this is not standard American, but in the earlier corpus there are enough instances to suggest that it was not abnormal for Shakespeare. The instances all have some sort of volitional element. Thus [73] may be paraphrased "if I should wish to say", and [74] is either "if I had not insisted on taking him at a word" or equivalent to "if I had not taken him at a word".

[73] What power is in Agrippa,
If I *would* say Agrippa, be it so,
To make this good? [AC II ii 163]

[74] and I had beene a man of any Occupation, if I *would* not haue taken him at a word, I would I might goe to Hell among the Rogues, [JC I ii 289]

Some miscellaneous items are worth mention. In [75][4] *would* inverts with the subject to express "if"; in [76] we can see the double use of phase marking that is increasingly frequent in PDE. [77] is of interest because *would* here is past as a result of sequence of tense forced by a nonexistent verb: that is, the past-tense "we expected that" is implied by the nominal "Our expectation". [78] represents the several (but fewer than those for *will*) instances of auxiliary with implied verb of motion, and the most fully marked verb phrase is in [79] with phase, voice, and negation. With "rather" there are two instances of *had* in place of today's (and Shakespeare's normal) hypothetical volitional *would* [80].

[75] Ah! *would* the scandall vanish with my life,
How happy then were my ensuing death? [R2 II i 69]
[76] yet who *would haue* thought the
old man to *haue* had so much blood in him [M V i 36]
[77] Our expectation that it *would* be thus
Hath made vs forward. [C III v 38]
[78] Reuenges burne in them: for their deere causes
Would to the bleeding, and the grim Alarme
Excite the mortified man. [M V ii 4]
[79] I *would* not haue been so fiddious'd, for
all the Chests in Carioles, and the Gold that's in them. [Co II i 130]
[80] I *had* rather heare (Lady) my Brach howle in Irish. [H4, 1 III i 254]

SHALL

The basic meaning of *shall* is today's "compulsive" meaning, in which *shall* expresses a prediction which is specifically backed up by the speaker's superior knowledge and/or authority. That is, the occurrence of the predication is assured "because I say so". This is by far the most frequent meaning of *shall* in the Shakespearian material, and it is well illustrated by [81].

[81] *Shall* I haue audience? he *shall* present *Hercules* in minoritie:
his *enter* and *exit shall* bee strangling a Snake; [LLL V i 142]

The other main meaning area is one of straight prediction like that of *will*. Today this meaning is essentially confined to "stylistic" *shall*, in which it appears with first-person

[4] Item [75] may well also represent a case of "noncontiguous syntactic haplology" for *'would that the scandal would vanish with my life', in which the two instances of *would* fall together. Syntactic haplology was discussed by W. Coates in "Syntactic Haplology", a paper read at the December, 1964, meeting of the Linguistic Society of America.

to indicate a privileged educational level. In the Elizabethan corpus there is no evidence for interpretation of predictive *shall* as stylistic; it occurs freely with all three persons, and first person instances appear freely in compulsive *shall*. The issue is much more a question of the difference, if any, between predictive *shall* and *will*; I can see none. There does seem to be a tendency to use a *shall* of different meaning from a nearby *will*, but this does not work perfectly. In [82] predictive *will* is followed by compulsive *shall*; in [83] the first and third *will*'s are volitional, the second *will* is predictive, and *shall* is compulsive; in [84] *will* has volitional elements and *shall* is predictive.

[82] To morrow then I *will* expect your comming,
To night I take my leaue, this naughtie man
Shall face to face be brought to *Margaret*, [MA V i 305]

[83] I may and *will*, if she be so contented:
She *will* be pleas'd, then wherefore should I doubt:
Hap what hap may, *Ile* roundly goe about her:
It *shall* goe hard if Cambio goe without her. [TS IV iv 108]

[84] *Adr*. Backe slaue, or I *will* breake thy pate a-crosse.
Dro. And he *will* blesse 'y crosse with other beating:
Betweene you, I *shall* haue a holy head. [CE II i 84]

On the other hand, there are a number of instances in which other factors may govern the use of one or the other: in [85] the present-day restriction that questions involving intention or willingness have *shall* in the first person and *will* in the others seems to be observed. To be sure, in both cases it is someone other than the speaker who is called on to produce the volition. In [86] *will* is time-neutral and *shall* adds a redundant emphasis to the time-futurity established by "tomorrow". On the other hand, there are several sentences, represented by [87], in which nothing at all can be seen to distinguish between *shall* and *will*.

[85] Heere comes Sir *Oliuer*: Sir *Oliuer Mar-text* you are wel met. *Will* you dispatch vs heere vnder this tree, or *shal* we go with you to your Chappell? [AYL III iii 57]

[86] No: 'tis not so deepe as a well, nor so wide as a Church doore, but 'tis inough, 't*will* serue: aske for me tomorrow, and you *shall* find me a graue man. [RJ III i 100]

[87] Pray do not Sir, I haue watch'd and trauail'd hard,
Some time I *shall* sleepe out, the rest *Ile* whistle:
A good mans fortune may grow out at heeles: [KL II ii 155]

Such sentences, together with the very existence of predictive *shall*, indicate at least the beginning of a decay in the consistent use and separate meaning of *shall*. Today that situation has progressed to the point where many speakers could get along without *shall* altogether. The confusion shows up clearly in [88], where the basic meanings of the two auxiliaries would seem to have been completely reversed. It also shows in

[89], in which the first *shall* is almost volitional; the second is predictive.

[88] and meet me in the palace wood, a mile without the Towne, by Moone-light, there we *will* rehearse: for if we meete in the Citie, we *shal*be dog'd with company, and our deuises knowne. [MND I ii 100]

[89] If you *shall* cleaue to my consent,
When 'tis, it *shall* make Honor for you. [M II i 25]

Time function for *shall* is almost always future; indeed time-neutral instances are so rare and strange-sounding that there is room for doubt as to whether reference to time function is even relevant for *shall* in such cases. There are only five time-neutral instances of *shall*, and all of them are predictive [90].

[90] You can play no part but Piramus, for Piramus is a sweet-fac'd man, a proper man as one *shall* see in a summers day; [MND I ii 83]

The essential futurity of *shall* appears very markedly in the thoroughly non-PDE use in time-clauses, as in [91]. Today an unmarked lexical verb would be used, instead of the explicit marking of futurity which the EMnE sentences provide.

[91] What will *Berowne* say when that he *shall* heare
Faith infringed, which such zeale did sweare. [LLL IV iii 146]

Predictive *shall* has one overtone: in [92] both *will* and *shall* are predictive-sequential. It seems very difficult to refer to compulsive *shall* as an overtone, since it is actually less marked than independent *shall* for force behind the assurance of occurrence. However, the great number of instances of compulsive *shall* make it impossible to consider the more marked meaning subordinate to the predictive, less marked one. Historically, of course, the development of a more generalized meaning from the more specific one is far from impossible, but it is hard to talk synchronically of one as subordinate to the other.

[92] If he be put vpon't, and that's as easie,
As to set Dogges on Sheepe, *will* be his fire
To kindle their dry Stubble: and their Blaze
Shall darken him for euer. [Co II i 290]

Such establishment of subordination is also made difficult by the existence of a number of items, all in the first person, which express intention much like that expressed by ambiguous *will*. As a matter of fact, in [93] we see both *will* and *shall* used this way, with no apparent difference of meaning. We can see that there are elements both of compulsive and of predictive *shall* in this example.

[93] Ile graffe it with you, and then I *shall* graffe it with a Medler: [AYL III ii 108]

In PDE, *should* has, essentially, two meanings. It may serve almost exclusively as a carrier of hypothesis – a function closely related to its origin as the past tense of *shall*. More commonly it may be what I have called "normative": paraphrased, this is something like "the predication conforms to the speaker's (or his delegate's) view of some aspect(s) of surrounding circumstance". This second meaning is less directly related to that of *shall*. It has one overtone, which expresses high probability.

In Shakespeare's plays these seem again to be the main divisions of meaning. The hypothetical instances divide into those which express pure conjecture and nothing else [94] – these are usually preceded by a subordinator like *if*, *that*, or *lest* – and those which are equivalent in meaning to *would* [95]. There are a surprising number of these, including a few examples of the sequential overtone [96].

[94] Ye Gods, it doth amaze me,
A man of such a feeble temper *should*
So get the start of the Maiesticke world,
And beare the Palme alone [JC I ii 140]

[95] O were fauoɹ so,
Your words I catch, faire Hermia ere I go,
My eare *should* catch your voice, my eye, your eye,
My tongue *should* catch your tongues sweet melodie, [MND I i 198]

[96] And I were so apt to quarrell as thou art, any man *should* buy the Fee-simple of my life, for an houre and a quarter. [RJ III i 33]

Normative *should* behaves as in today's English; one example will suffice [97]. Today's overtone of probability appears only once [98], but that is enough to establish its presence though not high frequency in EMnE.

[97] I am not so well as I *should* be: But Ile ne're out. [AC II vii 36]

[98] By all description this *should* be the place. [TA V iii 1]

In a number of cases the meanings of *shall* are simply past-marked, either for unreality or for past time. Past time instances are [99] for compulsive *shall* and [100] for predictive *shall*. Hypothetical instances include [101] for prediction, [102] for compulsive *shall*, and [103] for the *shall* of intention which combines authority and prediction.

[99] Your worship is deceiu'd, the gowne is made
Iust as my master had direction:
Grumio gaue order how it *should* be done. [TS IV iii 124]

[100] which rais'd in me
An vndergoing stomacke, to beare vp
Against what *should* ensue. [T I ii 184]

[101] If thou bee'st not damn'd for this, the diuell himselfe will haue no shepherds, I cannot see else how thou *shouldst* scape. [AYL III ii 76]

[102] There is a vice that most I doe abhorre,
And most desire *should* meet the blow of Iustice; [MM II ii 41]

[103] 'Tis spoken well:
Were we before our Armies, and to fight,
I *should* do thus. [AC II ii 33]

For both *shall* and *should* negation may, as in PDE, be either immediate or eventual, with no different effect on meaning. Phase-marked modals, whether normative [104] or predictive [105] are all contrary-to-fact. The last example, sentence [105], is the most fully marked verb phrase with *should*; all it lacks is the still rare aspect marking.

[104] Giue her the right you *should* haue giu'n her cosin,
And so dies my reuenge. [MA V i 300]

[105] And where I thought the remnant of mine age
Should haue beene cherish'd by her child-like dutie, [2G III i 74]

OUGHT

Ought appears twice in the corpus, once with the particle *to* and once without it. Both instances are negated. If there is any difference of meaning between *should* (normative) and *ought*, it is that *ought* refers exclusively to explicit social rules whereas *should* need not do so. However, there are so few instances of *ought* that the meaning difference may be attributable to coincidence [106], [107].[5]

[106] What, know you not
(Being Mechanicall) you *ought* not walke
Vpon a labouring day, without the signe
Of your Profession? [JC I i 5]

[107] Once if he do require our voyces, wee *ought* not *to* deny him. [Co II ii 187]

MUST

The present-day meaning of *must* is that the predication is required by some aspect or aspects of surrounding circumstance. The choice of aspect adds a little meaning of its own to the verb phrase, so it cannot be ignored, but there are enough different such aspects that a list incorporated into the definition would be cumbersome and overly specific. It is to be noted, however, that *must* is not necessarily marked for speaker's view. There is one derivative overtone which expresses the very high probability of the truth of the predication (sometimes instances of this are called "logical must)".

In Shakespeare's usage, the situation appears to be precisely the same. The majority of the occurrences express requirement of the predication by aspects of environment. Examples of such aspects are social necessity [108], legislation [109], exigencies of

[5] Examination of the 19 other occurrences of *ought* (*to*) in the rest of the plays of Shakespeare shows that in fact no difference seems to exist between normative *should* and *ought*. This is the PDE situation as well.

individual circumstances [110], laws of "nature" [111], logic [112], or individual make-up [113]. The basic meaning occasionally appears with the intensifying adverb *needs*.

[108] Therefore it *must* with circumstance be spoken
By one, whom she esteemeth as his friend. [2G III ii 37]

[109] But Valentine, if he be tane, *must* die. [2G III i 233]

[110] Goe not my Horse the better,
I *must* become a borrower of the Night,
For a darke houre, or twaine. [M III i 25]

[111] But small to greater matters *must* giue way. [AC II ii 14]

[112] if thou neuer saw'st good maners, then thy manners *must* be wicked, and wickednes is sin, and sinne is damnation: [AYL III ii 39]

[113] He cannot flatter he,
an honest mind and plaine, he *must* speake truth,
and they will take it so, if not, hee's plaine. [KL II ii 99]

he *must* speake truth, and hey will take it so, if not, hee's plaine. [KL II ii 99]

The overtone of probability, illustrated by [114][6] and [115] is usually the same as in PDE. There are two sentences, however, in which *must* is occurrential to an extent which it is not in PDE. In [116] and [117] *must* would today be expressed as "will have to". *Needs* in the latter again intensifies the element of requirement; this is the only instance where *needs* appears with the overtone of probability in *must*.

[114] and your Beards deserue not so honourable a graue, as to stuffe
a Botchers Cushion, or to be intomb'd in an Asses Packe-saddle;
yet you *must* bee saying, Martius is proud: [Co II i 88]

[115] No single soule
Can we set eye on: but in all safe reason
He *must* haue some Attendants. [C IV ii 177]

[116] My heart is great: but it *must* break with silence,
Er't be disburthen'd with a liberall tongue. [R2 II i 236]

[117] The King his Master, needs *must* take it ill
That he so slightly valued in his Messenger,
Should haue him thus restrained. [KL II ii 145]

Sentence [118] illustrates the difference between compulsive *shall* and *must*. It is essentially that, as stated above, *must* is not always marked for speaker's view of circumstances, while *shall* is heavily marked in this way. Negation of *must* is eventual.

[118] Not winde? it *shall*, it *must*, you see it doth. [H4,1 III i 108]

[6] Another interpretation of the *must* in this sentence is as a volitional with a meaning like "keep on", "insist on".

DARE

In PDE modal *dare* occurs twice, both times negated. It is treated as a marginal member of the modal class because of its infrequency and limited range of use. Its meaning, unchanged from Shakespeare's time, is something like "in the speaker's view the predication has no undesirable consequences". In PDE there is no marked past form.

Dare in the Shakespeare sample is far more frequent; it occurs 23 times [119]. Of these two are interrogative; five are negative; and two appear in *if*-clauses. The rest are positive (though several appear in fixed expressions like "I dare say. . ."). There are also three instances of non-modal *dares*, perhaps signaling a greater decay to come for *dare*. Nevertheless *dare* is fully modal and a firmly established member of the closed class in Shakespeare's system.

[119] And Protheus, we *dare* trust you in this kinde,
Because we know (on Valentines report)
You are already loues firme votary, [2G III ii 58]

Furthermore, there is a marked past-tense form *durst*, which appears seven times. However, the one unnegated instance of *durst* is in an *if*-clause, which indicates that *durst* is probably in less good standing as a modal than the present-tense form *dare*. *Durst* usually has past-time meaning, but in [120] the past marking carries hypothetical force.

[120] Neuer *durst* Poet touch a pen to write,
Vntill his Inke were tempred with Loues sighes: [LLL IV iii 346]

NEED

In the PDE corpus modal *need* appears four times, all negated. It, too, is marginal. The meaning is that the predication is required by the speaker's view of some aspect or aspects of the state of the world. There are many more catenative than modal instances of *need*.

The Shakespearian sample likewise has four instances of modal *need*, of which one is negative [121] and the other three are interrogative. They have the same meaning as in PDE. There are also two catenative instances, one without the *-s* which marks concord with a third-person singular subject [122] and three instances of negated, concord-marked *needs not* with unmarked infinitive. The evidence here points to *need* as a marginal modal used in limited environments in Shakespeare's time as today, with little change over the 300-year period.

[121] A speciall vertue: for then shee *neede* not be wash'd, and scowr'd. [2G III i 307]

[122] Why there is it: Come, sing me a bawdy Song,
make me merry: I was as vertuously giuen, as a
Gentleman *need* to be; [H4,1 III iii 16]

THE MODAL SYSTEM

We can conclude with Table 6, which is founded on the basic meanings. The farther to the right a meaning is located on the table, the more modal the auxiliary is. As in PDE, it looks as if there are two broad areas in which the meanings of the modals can differ, both of them affecting modality. Explanation of Table 7 is on pp. 75-77 above.

The only difference between the basic EMnE system and that of PDE is that PDE has only three rows instead of four, since *will*$_1$ is an overtone of the EMnE *will*$_2$ in PDE. Otherwise, as has been made evident throughout the paper, it looks as if the PDE modal semantic system was established by Shakespeare's time.

TABLE 6

The Modal System

		Contingency			
		required predication	non-occurrence not guaranteed	predication not prevented	predication conforms
Conditioner	environment	WILL$_2$	MAY$_1$	MAY$_2$ CAN	
	aspect of environment	MUST			
	speaker's view of environment	SHALL [NEED NOT]		DARE	SHOULD-OUGHT
	volition	WILL$_1$			

Appendix B

THE MODALS IN DRYDEN. A COMPARISON WITH SHAKESPEARE'S USAGE, AND, WHERE RELEVANT, WITH PRESENT-DAY ENGLISH

I. THE MATERIAL USED

For this brief comparison of Dryden and Shakespeare in the use of the modal auxiliaries, I have used the first three acts of *All for Love* (approximately 1,400 lines) and the first thirty pages of *An Essay of Dramatic Poesy*.[1] The one exception is that in *All for Love* (AFL) only the first two acts were used for examples of *will/would* because these modals are so frequent. Both samples must be considered slightly skewed; the play, like Shakespeare's plays, represents, at least for the characters, a unique and concrete sequence of events, so that future time function of *will* may be expected to appear very frequently. The *Essay*, on the other hand, is not only a generalized and relatively abstract work (thus leading us to expect a sizeable proportion of time-neutral instances of *will*), but it is also highly normative in nature, with the result that *must*, *ought* (*to*), and normative *should* have high frequencies.

II. COMPARISON

It proves convenient to compare Dryden's play with his prose at the same time as both are compared with Shakespeare's plays. The two asterisks ** enclose evidence that the grammar of AFL is more archaic than that of the *Essay*.

A. *Can*

Both AFL and the *Essay* show a smaller proportion of instances of *can* meaning "know how to" than Shakespeare. However, AFL shows the same equal proportions as Shakespeare of anything that can be called "internal" *can* to unmarked basic meanings, **but the *Essay* shows a much higher number of basic meanings than of internal ones.**

There are still no permissive instances of *can* or *could* in either of Dryden's works.

[1] Page references are all to Wm. Frost, ed., *Selected Works of John Dryden* (New York, Holt, Rhinehart, and Winston, 1953). *All for Love* occupies pages 92 to 174, and *An Essay of Dramatic Poesy* occupies pages 321-387.

Could outnumbers *can* in AFL but not in the *Essay*. However, since almost all instances of *could* in AFL are hypothetical rather than past-time, this imbalance is probably more a result of contextual skewness than of any violation of "Greenberg's Law" (marked forms are significantly less frequent than corresponding unmarked forms).[2]

B. *May*

The behavior of *may* in AFL is closer to that of *may* in Shakespeare than is that of *may* in the *Essay*. As in Shakespeare, the most frequent meaning for *may* in AFL is the circumstantial one, while in the prose selection occurrential, balanced, and circumstantial *may* all have approximately equal frequencies. For *might* there seems to be little change: occurrence is the most frequent dimension in both Dryden selections as it is in Shakespeare. *May/might* remains less frequent than *can, could, will, would*, and *should.*

C. *Will*

As noted above, the most striking thing about *will* in Dryden is that in AFL, as in Shakespeare's plays, almost all the instances of *will* have future time function, whereas for the *Essay* the clear majority are time-neutral. This corresponds with the predictions made from the types of context involved and cannot be correlated with historical change. Another difference, this time between all of Dryden and Shakespeare, that cannot be correlated with the intervening interval of 75 years between the two writers is the total absence of time-neutral *will* of characterization (which appeared in Shakespeare and which is normal in PDE). The absence in Dryden is probably accidental.

Considerably more significant is the fact that *will* is much less frequently volitional in the prose *Essay* than it is in the Dryden play. The statistics for the meanings of *will* in AFL are much like those for Shakespeare, but those of the *Essay* resemble the PDE situation more closely. However, both of Dryden's works show not only more time-neutral instances of *would* than any other kind, but also, as second in frequency only to predictives, the time-neutral volitionals in which the originally hypothetical meaning of the past tense is lost, leaving only a slightly more deferential volitional. Here both play and prose are closer to Shakespeare than to PDE [1].

[1] But, if he *would* have us to imagine, that in exalting one character the rest of them are neglected, . . . [*Essay*, p. 349]

[2] From lectures given in the series *Trends in Linguistics*, summer, 1964, at Indiana University, on linguistic universals. Greenberg's lectures are forthcoming in *Current Trends in Linguistics*, Volume III: *Theoretical Foundation*, ed. C. A. Ferguson (The Hague, Mouton & Co.), under the title "Problems in the Study of Universals".

D. *Shall*

**It is in *shall/should* that we see the most dramatic change. AFL has many occurrences of *shall* of all kinds (though mostly independent), whereas the *Essay* has only four. Although normative *should* predominates in both Dryden's play and his *Essay*, only in AFL does *should* also appear as the marked past form of predictive *shall* [2]. This may be for no other reason than the fact that there are significantly more instances of *shall* than *should* in the play; at any rate *should* in both the Shakespeare plays and AFL appears to be felt as a past-tense form still, in contrast both with the *Essay* and with PDE usage.

[2] Your arms *should* open, even without your knowledge,
To clasp them in; your feet *should* turn to wings,
To bear you to them; and your eyes dart out
And aim a kiss, ere you could reach the lips. [AFL, III, 248]

In the *Essay* the situation looks much more like American PDE. *Should* is much more frequent than the rare *shall* and divides into essentially the same meaning groups as in PDE: normative and pure hypothetical.**

Both of Dryden's selections differ from Shakespeare in one particular. This is that straight predictive *would* is not used with the first person singular; instead *should* is always used. "Stylistic" *shall/should* did not appear in Shakespeare, nor does there seem to be any evidence for stylistic conditioning of the unmarked-tense forms *will* and *shall* in Dryden. Since even in Dryden's prose *shall* does not yet seem to be used as a stylistic device, perhaps without the prescriptive grammarians' rule predictive *shall* might eventually have gone out of use altogether.

In neither of Dryden's works does *should* invert with the subject to make the protasis of a conditional as in Shakespeare and PDE. **The only modal to do this is *could*, which does it 6 times in the play and only once in the prose.**

E. *Ought* (*to*)

Ought (*to*) for the most part shows no change in meaning from Shakespeare's time; it is still pretty much equivalent to all of normative *should* except any residual hypothetical element in the latter. *Ought* appears twice in AFL, both times as a propredicate without *to*. This is proportionally much more than the twice it appears in the Shakespeare corpus, but still nothing to the one propredicate *ought* and the eleven full instances of *ought to* in the *Essay*. **While the frequency of *ought to* may be attributable to the skewness of the sample, as mentioned above, the considerable difference in frequency still seems to me to argue significantly for the greater modernity of Dryden's prose as opposed to his play.**

F. *Must*

Must remains in meaning the same as in Shakespeare. In Dryden there are no instances of the overtone of probability at all, though there is one instance in AFL where the meaning certainly approaches probability [3]. The absence of the overtone is probably fortuitous, since probability both with normative *should* and with *must* is definitely as much part of PDE as of Shakespeare's EMnE.

[3] My life on't, he still drags a chain along
That needs *must* clog his flight. [AFL, II, 91].

One type of requirement expressed by *must* in Dryden but not in Shakespeare, is one equivalent to "cannot not + verb". This is illustrated by [4].

[4] I cannot: If I could, those thoughts were vain.
Faithless, ungrateful, cruel, though he be,
I still *must* love him. [AFL, II, 33]

G. *Dare* and *Need*

***Dare* and *durst* both appear in AFL, in about the same proportions as they did in Shakespeare. In the *Essay*, however, *dare* does not appear in the first thirty pages; it appears only three times in the entire *Essay*; and *durst* is not used at all.** Positive *dare* is still used by Dryden in both selections.

Need is used five times in AFL and five in the entire *Essay*. It is always negated, either directly or indirectly. The figures represent something of an increase compared to Shakespeare's four occurrences in a rather larger corpus. We may conclude that *need* has gained some strength in 75 years.

III. CONCLUSIONS

The most interesting aspect of this study was less the difference between Dryden and Shakespeare than the difference between Dryden's drama and his prose. The use of the modals in AFL was almost exactly like that of Shakespeare, while the usage in the *Essay* was in many ways much more similar to that of PDE. The meanings of the modals have not changed (except that in the *Essay* we are now justified in calling volition in *will* an overtone of prediction), but the frequencies of the various meanings have.

This conclusion of the greater modernity of the *Essay* is supported by one thing in particular: in the prose appear three catenatives, while in AFL there were no catenatives at all. There were none in Shakespeare. The catenatives in the *Essay* are *going to* [5] (also pp. 358, 372), *be to* [6] (also pp. 327, 331), and *used to* [7]. *Be to* is fairly

TABLE 7

Frequencies of Meanings in Dryden

	play	prose
CAN	27	28
basic meaning	13	22
know (how to)	3	1
internal	10	5
occurrential	1	—
COULD	34	8
basic meaning, hypothetical	10	3
basic meaning, past	3	2
know (how to), hypothetical	3	—
know (how to), past	1	—
internal, hypothetical	12	—
internal, past	1	1
occurrential, hypothetical	4	—
MAY	16	21
permissive	2	1
circumstantial	8	7
balanced	1	6
occurrential	5	7
MIGHT	8	8
circumstantial, hypothetical	1	—
circumstantial, past	1	2
balanced, hypothetical	1	1
balanced, past	1	—
occurrential, hypothetical	4	3
occurrential, past	—	2
WILL	54	14
sequential, future	3	—
sequential, neutral	—	—
basic, future	16	6
basic, neutral	2	23
volitional, future	19	1
volitional, neutral	4	1
ambiguous: volitional or predictive:		
future	9	2
neutral	—	1
WOULD	46	26
basic meaning		
future, hypothetical	3	—
neutral, hypothetical	15	17
future, past	1	1
volitional		
future, hypothetical	2	—
future, past	2	1
neutral, past	2	—
volitionals in which the hypothetical meaning of past tense is lost		
future	6	—
neutral	13	6
ambiguous: volitional or predictive		
future, past	—	1
SHALL	31	4
compulsive	26	1
predictive	2	1
predictive, compulsive	1	1
predictive, future	—	1
predictive, neutral	1	—
predictive, sequential	1	—
SHOULD	21	20
compulsive, hypothetical	1	1
compulsive, past	1	—
pure hypothesis	4	8
normative, neutral	12	9
normative, future	1	—
predictive, hypothetical	—	—
predictive, past	1	—
stylistic	1	2
OUGHT	2	12
with *to*	—	11
without *to*	2	1
MUST	28	16
required	27	16
probability	1	—
DARE	7	—
DURST	2	—
NEED	5	1

* There were five instances of NEED in the entire *Essay*.

frequent; in the past tense it is probably used as one substitute for *must*, which cannot be marked for past. The absence of *have to* has one interesting effect. Phase is also used to mark basic-meaning *must* for past time [8]; to speakers of PDE this looks peculiar because we would say "had to" and reserve phase for use with the overtone of high probability.

[5] Eugenius was *going to* continue this discourse, when Lisideius told him that it was necessary, before they proceeded further, to take a standing measure of their controversy; [*Essay*, p. 327]

[6] . . . so that they set the audience, as it were, at the post where the race *is to* be concluded; [*Essay*, p. 330]

[7] . . . as the women in Juvenal's time *used to* cry out in the fury of their kindness. [*Essay*, p. 342]

[8] . . . had he lived in our age, or in his own could have writ with our advantages, no man but *must* have yielded to him; [*Essay*, p. 342]

BIBLIOGRAPHY

PRIMARY SOURCE

A Standard Sample of Present-Day English for Use with Digital Computers, ed. W. N. Francis. Magnetic Tape. (Providence, 1963-1964. Full details about the contents and format are included in an accompanying *Manual* published at Brown University in 1964).

SECONDARY SOURCES

Curme, George O., *Syntax* (= *A Grammar of the English Language*, vol. III), (Boston, D. C. Heath and Co., 1931).

Diver, William, "The Modal System of the English Verb", *Word*, XX, (1964), 322-52.

Fries, Charles C., *The Structure of English* (New York, Harcourt, Brace, and Co., 1952).

Jakobson, Roman, *Shifters, Verbal Categories, and the Russian Verb* (Russian Language Project, Harvard University, Department of Slavic Languages and Literatures, 1957).

Jespersen, Otto, *A Modern English Grammar on Historical Principles* (London, Allen and Unwin, Ltd., 1961).

Jespersen, Otto, *Negation in English and Other Languages* (= *Det Køl. Danske Kidenskabernes Selskab, Historisk-filologiske Meddelelser*, I, 5) (Copenhagen, Andr. Fred Høst & Søn, 1917).

Joos, Martin, *The English Verb: Form and Meanings* (Madison, University of Wisconsin, 1963), preliminary edition.

Joos, Martin, *The English Verb: Form and Meanings* (Madison, University of Wisconsin Press, 1964).

Long, Ralph B., *The Sentence and Its Parts* (Chicago, University of Chicago Press, 1961).

Marckwardt, Albert H., and Walcott, Fred, *Facts about Current English Usage* (National Council of Teachers of English, New York, D. Appleton-Century Co., 1938).

A New English Dictionary on Historical Principles, ed. Sir J. A. H. Murray, H. Bradley, W. A. Craigie, C. T. Onions (Oxford, 1888, 1928). Abbreviated as OED.

Poutsma, H., *A Grammar of Late Modern English*, Parts I, II, and III (Groningen, P. Noordhoff, 1929).

Quirk, Randolph, *The Use of English* (New York, St. Martin's Press, 1962).

Strang, Barbara M. H., *Modern English Structure* (London, Edward Arnold, Ltd., 1962).

Twaddell, W. F., *The English Verb Auxiliaries*, Second ed., rev. (Providence, Brown University Press, 1963).

Whitehall, Harold, *Structural Essentials of English* (New York, Harcourt, Brace, and Co., 1952).

Zandvoort, R. W., *A Handbook of English Grammar*, Second ed. (London, Longmans, Green, and Co., 1962).

COMMENTS ON ARTICLES IN THE BIBLIOGRAPHY

Curme, *Jespersen* (1961), *Poutsma*, and *Zandvoort:*

Within the terminology and certain conceptual limits of "traditional" grammar, these representatives of the so-called "scholarly grammarians" give exhaustive and detailed discussions of all the modals. However, substantive points and examples are scattered and not systematically arranged from the point of view of the student of the modals because they come up as corollaries or illustrations of points made in a different system of reference, e.g. of a throughgoing indicative-subjunctive opposition. In Curme's case, this sometimes leads to forced interpretations of material.

Because of this difference of outlook and organization, worthwhile insights and important data sometimes fail to be treated in an organized way and desirable generalizations are not made. Zandvoort in particular seems also to look at and treat the modals as troublesome translation points for the non-native reader of English, though he attempts nothing of a contrastive nature. All four refer to a "future tense" of which *will* is an exponent.

Diver:

This article is a very incoherent piece of thinking and writing. The style is pretentious and turgid; the data are manhandled to make minor and in the long run irrelevant points; large systematic generalities are ignored in favor of small and unrelated ones. The principle of Occam's Razor is ignored everywhere.

Fries:

This book is concerned almost exclusively with syntactic and morphological structure of English. It makes occasional statements about usage but has nothing about semantics or semantic system.

Jespersen (1917):

There are some interesting comments here on the negation relationship between *must* and permissive *may*, and on a few other points.

Joos (1964):

I have relied heavily on this book for its treatment of the verb phrase as a whole, particularly for its treatment of tense. However, while there are important insights and many places of agreement between my discussion and that of Joos in his last chapter, on modal meanings, in many cases the very neat and apparently inclusive logical systems proposed are in a way too good to be true. Much of this perfectly fitting three-dimensional system covers the data adequately, but for where it seems to break down there appears to be some subtle distortion so that system seems to take precedence over fact. The difference between the British English of Joos' perhaps too limited corpus and the American of mine does not account for all of my disagreements with his treatment.

The points are usually clearly and coherently made; many of them are valid and very interesting; and all of them are stimulating. So far this and the Diver article are the only published treatments of the modals and their system as primary centers of interest.

Long:

Long sometimes slips into the same pitfall as Curme by forcing the facts into a "traditional" framework instead of letting them speak for themselves. He tends to be concerned with style and usage problems and shows little interest in systematic treatment of meaning. There are some accurate insights.

Marckwardt and Walcott:

Concerned entirely with opinions on such standard questions as usage of *shall* and *will*, this book is useful as a supplement but contributes little else.

Oxford English Dictionary:

Needless to say, the OED treatments of the meanings of the modals are carefully organized and comprehensive. There is no attempt at isolating semantic lowest common denominators, however, and sometimes the entries reflect the educationally acquired biasses of the editors.

Quirk:

Discussion of the modals is infrequent and superficial, appearing only as the modals relate to other matters. *Will* and *shall* are classified as modally tinged future tense.

Strang:

As the title of her book indicates, Strang treats the modals as elements in the verb phrase structure. Treatment of meaning is for the most part occasional and unsystematic, though each modal is named as a manifestation of one of a set of moods; thus *will* establishes a mood of determination. Questions of usage, especially of *will* and *shall*, receive attention.

Twaddell:

This is a clear, concise, and perceptive treatment of everything it touches upon. Its range is rather restricted, so that there is not a deep investigation of modal semantics and systems of meaning. Meaning is treated as most relevant as it affects the sometimes unusual, always useful points of usage brought up.

Whitehall:

For this book, as for Quirk, the modals are of peripheral interest and are discussed only occasionally and superficially.

JANUA LINGUARUM

STUDIA MEMORIAE NICOLAI VAN WIJK DEDICATA

Edited by C. H. van Schooneveld

SERIES PRACTICA

1. MARILYN CONWELL and ALPHONSE JUILLAND: Louisiana French Grammar, I: Phonology, Morphology, and Syntax. 1963. 207 pp., 2 maps. Cloth. Gld. 36.—
3. IRENE GARBELL: The Jewish Neo-Aramaic Dialects of Persian Azerbaijan: Linguistic Analysis and Folkloristic Texts. 1965. 342 pp., map. Cloth. Gld. 64.—
4. MORRIS F. GOODMAN: A Comparative Study of Creole French Dialects. 1964. 143 pp., map. Gld. 22.—
5. ROLAND HARWEG: Kompositum und Katalysationstext, vornehmlich im späten Sanskrit. 1964. 164 pp. Gld. 25.—
6. GUSTAV HERDAN: The Structuralistic Approach to Chinese Grammar and Vocabulary: Two Essays. 1964. 56 pp., 4 figs. Gld. 18.—
7. ALPHONSE JUILLAND: Dictionnaire Inverse de la Langue Française. 1965. 564 pp., 9 figs. Cloth. Gld. 80.—
8. A. HOOD ROBERTS: A Statistical Linguistic Analysis of American English. 1965. 437 pp., 11 figs., 6 tables. Cloth. Gld. 54.—
9. VALDIS LEJNIEKS: Morphosyntax of the Homeric Greek Verb. 1964. 92 pp. Gld. 15.—
10. ROBERT E. DIAMOND: The Diction of the Anglo-Saxon Metrical Psalms. 1963. 59 pp. Gld. 10.—
11. JOSEPH E. GRIMES: Huichol Syntax. 1964. 105 pp. Gld. 18.—
12. CLARA N. BUSH: Phonetic Variation and Acoustic Distinctive Features: A Study of Four General American Fricatives. 1964. 161 pp., 64 figs., 84 tables. Gld. 30.50
13. WILLIAM E. CASTLE: The Effect of Selective Narrow-Band Filtering on the Perception of Certain English Vowels. 1964. 209 pp., 53 figs., 84 tables. Gld. 38.—
14. ANN SHANNON: A Descriptive Syntax of the Parker Manuscript of the Anglo-Saxon Chronicle from 734-891. 1964. 68 pp. Gld. 13.—
15. EICHI KOBAYASHI: The Verb Forms of the *South English Legendary*. 1964. 87 pp. Gld. 17.—
16. HOMER L. FIRESTONE: Description and Classification of Sirionó, a Tupí-Guaraní Language. 1965. 70 pp., 7 figs. Gld. 18.—
17. WOLF LESLAU: Ethiopian Argots. 1964. 65 pp. Gld. 16.—
21. ERICA REINER: A Linguistic Analysis of Akkadian. 1966. 155 pp., graph. Gld. 30.—
23. MARVIN K. MAYERS (ed.), Languages of Guatemala. 1966. 318 pp. Gld. 40.—

MOUTON & CO · PUBLISHERS · THE HAGUE